The Silent Psychopath

Why you should never date someone
you meet in rehab

By Jennylee Rose Bruno

The Silent Psychopath

Copyright © 2019 Jennylee Rose Bruno

ALL RIGHTS RESERVED

Published by JJSB Publishing LLC

ISBN: 978-168454983-2

Printed in the United States of America

Except as permitted under the United States Copyright Act of 1976, no part of this publication may be reproduced or distributed in any form or by any means, or stored in a database or retrieval system, without prior written permission of the publisher.

*I dedicate this story to my five children:
John, David, Kaylee,
Karalyn and Brandon*

What is a Psychopath?

Psychopaths are callous and show no empathy. They have no concern for the feelings of others. They have weak connections in their brain's emotional systems and high thresholds for disgust. They show a lack of emotion, particularly of shame, guilt, and embarrassment and are notorious for their lack of fear.

When normal people anticipate something painful will happen, a brain network activates; they sweat and their heart rate increases. In psychopaths this brain network shows no activity.

Psychopaths blame others for events that are their fault. They lie with a straight face and exude charm and glibness. They do not show the same brain response to emotional cues that normal people do. They have a grandiose sense of self-worth and are very impulsive. Hence they are prone to drug abuse and other risk-taking behavior.

They are pathologically egocentric and live parasitic lifestyles. They are carefree, cunningly manipulative, promiscuous and unable to plan for the future. They have no realistic long-term goals, a low tolerance to frustration and are easily provoked into violence.

All I Want

I just want to be loved

I felt unloved my whole life

I keep searching for that true love

Having that love from someone is like magic

True love takes the pain away from my heart

I got too much pain in my heart

True love heals my heart like gold

Someone please love me for who I am

True love is my destiny

Jennylee Rose Bruno

Preface

A huge explosion sent my body flying back sharply. The noise was so intense I felt my hearing aid crack. Then I sensed something looping in a circle near my heart and lungs like a rollercoaster before quickly disappearing from my body.

I was confused for a few seconds. Then I remember staring directly at the barrel of gun that was aimed at me, noticing whispy curls of smoke floating from the end and the smell of burning. There's no way I'd had been shot. I couldn't have been. This was too surreal.

Then every moment became a slow motion movie segment with me screaming, "No!" I turned to look behind me to see where the bullet had gone. There was a huge Jackson Pollock splatter of red across the white wall. Then I looked down.

My beautiful white pajamas were quickly becoming dyed bright red from the warm running waterfall of blood that was pouring out of me. Was this is really happening? I realized I was dying slowly.

I forced my brain to keep working by thinking about my parents and my only brother, grasping hold of memories from my childhood to keep myself alive. I didn't want to die right now. I still wanted a family of my own and lots of children.

Fearing that he wasn't done because I was still breathing, I told him I'd say it was just an accident and promised that he wouldn't get into trouble... automatically lying to protect myself and my family, just as I had for so many years...

Chapter 1

I have never told anyone this story, including my family, friends, doctors, police detectives or psychiatrists. I especially haven't shared it with my mother. I was so used to her brushing me off and knew she wouldn't take me seriously.

I don't know why I've never told anybody. Maybe I was ashamed I had got involved with such a monster. Was that the best I could do? I was tall and slim with long dark hair. I made men's heads turn. I could have held out for a genuine sweetheart. Instead, I settled for a demented psychopath who used me for his pleasure and controlled me with terror when I was just a teenager.

He took away my happiness and kept me captive at gunpoint day and night for four years. My life was dictated by my wristwatch. He allowed me fifteen minutes, not a second more, to run a quick errand. If I didn't return in time he said he'd kill someone or something I loved. He also brainwashed me into believing the police wouldn't help me.

Back in the 1980s there was no technology such as cellphones, iPads, computers or Facebook. There were just landlines and phone booths. People sent letters and read newspapers.

Teenagers had pen friends, read books, listened to vinyl records and watched TV in their bedroom. It was a wonderful, simple life in many ways. But it also allowed terrible things to happen behind closed doors.

Being deaf meant I was even more isolated, trying to figure out what life was about. Information about domestic violence and mental disorders that was available to the hearing world was silent to me.

As a result of an almost deadly shooting, I was prescribed morphine, Oxycontin and Demerol, so I was able to subdue most of the memories for many years. Today I still have excruciating pain in my shoulder and fibromyalgia, which is like been drenched in agony from head to toe. I'm also physically exhausted and mentally wrecked most days. Depression doesn't describe it. Sometimes I wish I could sleep and never wake up.

Ever since my ordeal I have forced myself to focus on being a good wife and mother, although I realize with terrible regret that some of the things that happened to me have affected my five children very badly.

I'll never forget the hours I spent in the half-darkness with a gun that was pointed at my heart or between my eyes. I'd have to lie very still and not turn over no matter how painful it was being in the same position. I couldn't go to the bathroom either, because he'd threaten to shoot me if I moved an inch.

Years afterwards I was afraid of sleeping alone. I'd wake up in a sweat with the sheets tangled around my legs from all the tossing and turning. I had deep lines between my eyes and furrows across my forehead from the nightmares. I needed Botox at an early age. My teeth cracked because I clenched my jaws so hard in my sleep. I've spent thousands of dollars on dental work. I went through a hell like no one should experience and I was in and out of psychiatric hospitals in the late 1990s because I was obsessed with killing myself.

Then one day I realized I wasn't crazy. I didn't have a psychiatric illness like schizophrenia. I didn't hallucinate or have bipolar disorder. I was just replaying the past over and over in my mind.

I remember that day of realization vividly. There were two nurses behind the desk making notes on the patients under their supervision. I looked around and tried to figure out what was wrong with them myself.

There was one frail old lady in her seventies with shoulder-length white hair. Her frowning face was filled with wrinkles and it looked like she hadn't taken care of herself her entire life. She was pacing the hallway and muttering under her breath. I put her problems down to decades of sadness and street drugs.

Another lady in her forties was sitting across from me in a huge recliner, reading a book. Why was she here? She was so young, calm and normal looking. A nurse came over with a plastic tray loaded with pills in plastic cups. There was my answer.

Then I heard a nurse shouting in the distance (I can make out loud noises with my hearing aids). Two technicians ran to her aid. A boy, I'm guessing eighteen years old, was running naked down the hallway. He was as skinny as a rail with an unshaven face. His greasy auburn hair was sticking up and you could see his privates amidst a huge reddish bush. The technicians tried to get him back to his room using restraints.

At that moment something snapped inside my mind. I wasn't like any of the people in here. I told myself, *Jennylee, you're not going to throw your life in the trash can. You only get one chance and that's it.* I checked myself out and never went to another mental facility again. That's how I escaped.

But why was I there in the first place?

This is a true story about my life. A story I have kept secret for over thirty years.

Chapter 2

I was born in a hospital in Putnam, Connecticut on May 6th, 1968. My parents, Joseph and Janice Bruno, were proud of their first baby girl and named me Jennifer. When I was about two years old, a family friend noticed I didn't respond when they called my name. Around this age I almost got hit by a car because I couldn't hear my parents screaming. Thankfully my mother ran out and pulled me off the edge of the sidewalk before I was run over. That's when my parents took me to an audiologist to get my hearing tested and it was discovered that I was profoundly deaf in both ears. My parents remembered that I had reacted to the sound of a vacuum cleaner when I was about six months old, but after I was sick with a high fever I didn't notice it anymore.

My mother had a hard time accepting I was deaf and was distressed about it for a long time. To help her deal with the trauma of my disability she decided to treat me like a normal hearing child.

A few months after my diagnosis, the deaf actor, Bernard Bragg, visited the house and encouraged my parents to learn basic sign language. He said it was important to start as soon as possible as it would help me understand English. He played with me on the lawn on a blanket and used sign language, forming words like 'milk,' 'play' and 'toys.' I replied back, having learned quickly by watching him sign. My parents were shocked I picked it up so fast. Bernard left them with a copy of his book on signing, which they still have to this day.

My father worked hard as a blue-collar worker, raising a family on a limited budget. He bought a ranch house in the suburbs in Danbury, Connecticut. When I was five he was transferred and we moved to Duxbury, Massachusetts to an enormous three-story, gray colonial property on a private street in an affluent neighborhood. It had a gray picket fence and a yard filled with red rosebushes.

I ran inside to pick my bedroom, shouting, "Mine! Mine! Mine!" I chose one at the front of the house with a huge walk-in closet. My brother, Antonio, who is one year younger than me, got the bedroom opposite, down the hallway.

My parents didn't want me to go to the local deaf school. They wanted me to pretend I was like everyone else. So I'd wait for the bus with the hearing kids and went to a regular school every day. Mom and Dad had visited the local deaf boarding school and didn't like it because they wouldn't see me every day. The sight of a lone teddy bear on a twin-sized bed in the dormitory was just too sad for my mother so she refused to let me attend, even though it would have been perfect for me.

My father came from a strong-willed Italian family and grew up in Boston's North End in a tight-knit Italian neighborhood. His parents, James and Eleanor Bruno, owned a delicatessen called 'Bruno's' in the corner of the historic Faneuil Hall.

Grammy Bruno was the best Italian cook ever and made everything from scratch, including pasta, marinara sauce, stuffed lobster, lasagna, chicken cordon bleu, cookies and desserts. I'd always look forward to going to their house for Sunday dinner. They lived in a white two-story brick house in the center of Boston. Airplanes would fly directly over their roof. Sometimes the noise was so intense the windows would rattle, which I could hear when my hearing aids were on. When I was a teenager they had double glazing put in for free by the city of Boston.

Down in the basement, the pale-green rough-plastered walls were lined with wooden shelves stacked with Italian food cans and rows of metal boxes full of 100%-pure Italian olive oil. They had a white chest freezer next to a huge red pool table. Me, my brother and our cousins, Kristen and Jamie, would sneak ice cream sandwiches all the time. The freezer would be empty by the time we left, but was always replenished before we returned.

We'd play at that pool table for hours or make a fort out of the two dark-red love seats, while the grown-ups sat at the table nearby eating shrimp appetizers and prosciutto wrapped around long skinny breadsticks, drizzled with olive oil. There was always plenty of food in the house because my grandparents would bring home any unsold products from their store. Their sign, 'J. Bruno & Co Meat Products', still hangs proudly on the red-brick wall in the food court at Faneuil Hall Marketplace in Boston.

My Uncle Jimmy and his wife Nancy became my godparents through the Catholic Church. Uncle Jimmy was a funny guy who owned a successful car dealership and always drove a brand-new

Corvette. He lived in a huge house with a swimming pool in the Boston area. Whenever we'd visit I'd run to the enormous games room with all its pinball machines and black leather stools and play on them for hours.

My mother Janice's family was the opposite of my father's. They were of English descent and lived on farms out in the country in Barre, Massachusetts. My mother's family wasn't close because her father was an alcoholic who was cruel to my mother, the youngest of his kids. Grandmother Bertha remained loyally married to him for years, but when my mom told her she couldn't take me to the house when I was a baby because of his drinking, she filed for divorce.

Consequently, I never had a relationship with my grandfather except when I met him once when I was about twelve. My mother drove me and my brother to see him. He was living above an old saloon bar. He had the most beautiful piercing blue eyes I'd ever seen, but the skin on his face was loose, like an English bulldog. He went down to the bar and brought me a warm ginger ale with a dead fly in it. I couldn't really understand him because he mumbled, so I couldn't read his lips and had to ask my mother to repeat what he was saying. When it was time to say goodbye, I looked into his intensely blue eyes and saw he was overcome with emotion, probably because he knew he'd never see us again. I cried all the way home. It was sad to see someone love his alcohol so much that he didn't get to see his family.

I adored my Grandmother Bertha. She was always so patient, calm and stoic. She was very loving towards to me growing up and I never once saw her get angry. She made the best out of a hard situation and was very humble. If problems arose she accepted them and moved on without feeling sorry for herself or getting annoyed with anyone. That was amazing to me. I wanted to be just like her. Grandmother Bertha wore wire-rimmed glasses and an old-fashioned flower-print apron all the time because she was always cleaning and cooking. She would bake pies and cookies and make pastry from scratch, flattening it out with her rolling pin. Her old farmhouse reminded me of Dorothy's in *The Wizard of Oz*. It had a Victorian roll-top bathtub with lions-claw feet and the floorboards squeaked when you went upstairs. The bedrooms were full of antique furniture and travel chests crammed with letters, postcards, dresses and hats.

Her son, my Uncle Pete, lived with her his entire life and never got married. I think it was because he already felt safe and content. He was very tall at six feet four inches and owned a logging business, cutting trees for a living. He wore the same red plaid shirt, heavy-duty khaki pants and a hunter hat every day. When he came home he'd take off his boots and put them next to the stove to dry. The whole house would smell like a pine forest. Everything in the house had to stay exactly the same because my uncle had obsessive compulsive disorder. Dinner was at six o'clock and no later. The hand mirror had to be set to the left and the comb placed four inches away on the bathroom vanity. If I moved it or accidentally knocked it out of line someone would put it back in its proper place.

In the fall I'd climb inside his timber lorry and pretend I was a logger. Then I'd help him load the logs, wearing oversized gloves to protect myself from splinters. We loved doing deliveries because it was fun passing the logs to each other from the truck. He'd even drive two hours to our house and leave some in our garage.

Our house in Duxbury had a wood stove on the porch where we'd eat dinner. I'd read my book sitting in the wicker chair next to its warmth. Sometimes we'd all sit out there and play Scrabble. Mom would make hot drinks in a big pot, with cinnamon sticks floating on the top. I can still smell its spicy scent lingering in the air. I used to love sitting in that wicker rocking chair, reading and occasionally looking out to the backyard through the screened doors. There'd be a foot of snow on the deck, yet there would be red robins and blue jays pecking at the bird feeder high up on its stand in our backyard. I felt so safe and content and was lucky to enjoy such a happy and secure upbringing.

On Saturday mornings my dad would get up early and make us all a breakfast of scrambled eggs, bacon and toast to give my mother a break from cooking all week. The smell of the bacon would wake me up early. Sometimes he'd bring us a box from Dunkin' Donuts on Sunday mornings. I loved the lemon donuts with powdered sugar and the fresh, gooey Boston cream donuts bursting with vanilla custard.

But I hated going to Catholic Church, which started at 10am. I'd sit on the uncomfortable pew and watch everyone, studying their faces to try to figure out what their lives were about. I'd say to my mother, "That person isn't happy with her husband and she'll get divorced ... That person is depressed ... That person is mad at someone ..."

I was right every time. My mother would talk to the church gossips and update me, saying, "Oh my goodness, you can read people's emotions and know what's going on with them!" The only reason I paid so much attention was because I didn't understand a word the priest was saying and I was bored.

Eventually I could even gauge when my mother was upset. I'd ask, "What's wrong with you? Why are you angry?" She ended up shielding her face so I couldn't read her moods.

When I was about thirteen I told my parents I didn't want to go to church anymore. I hated sitting on the hard, wooden pew not knowing what was going on. From that day on I was allowed to stay at home. About six months later my dad stopped going as a show of solidarity and because his free time was too precious to spend doing something he wasn't passionate about like my mom.

Dad enjoyed spending that extra time with me on Sundays. That's how we developed our close bond. He bought a sailboat so we could go to the ocean and explore the coast. He hitched it to his Jeep and took us to Duxbury Beach. I loved sailing. It was so peaceful out on the water with nobody making fun of me for my speech problems and deafness. He took me fishing at Duxbury Bridge to catch flounders. He'd fillet them and cook them in seasoned flour and olive oil in his square electric skillet. That fish was so delicious. I also enjoyed accompanying him on clam-digging trips to Duxbury Bay Beach. I'd wear my oldest sneakers and clothes because the mud was so black and stinky.

I'd go out into the water and feel around for shells that were unopened and put them in my wire basket.

One day my Grandpa Bruno joined us. He got his feet stuck in the mud and had water up to his knees. Then he fell forwards, screaming, "Help, help!" My dad and I pulled him back up straight. He had black sticky mud all over him. I couldn't stop laughing. Traveling back, he had to sit in the back of the Jeep with all the windows down and the sunroof open because he smelled so bad. When we got home Dad hosed him down from top to toe. Everyone thought it was hilarious. Dad boiled the clams in a huge pot. Then he filled some coffee mugs with hot water and gave us each a small glass bowl full of melted butter. We dipped the cooked clams in the hot water and then dunked them in the butter. They tasted like heaven.

When my dad was reading on the couch I'd snuggle up against him and give him dozens of kisses on his cheeks and lots of hugs. He gave me lots of attention and spent hours with me because I think he knew I was struggling at school.

He had a good friend, Tom, who worked for the Secret Service at the White House in Washington D.C. I was impressed by Tom because he was a bodyguard to the President of the United States. I even saw him on television when President Reagan was fired at on the golf course.

We all took a trip to Washington D.C. to see the White House and learn about its history. I was so excited because Tom had arranged for a private tour of the building at night time. It was one of the highlights of my life. I felt so special. Dad drove up to the security gates and repeated the code that Tom had given him.

The four security staff directed us down a long hallway with dark-blue carpet. The walls were lined with gold-framed portraits. I even saw the door to President Reagan's personal 'Barber Shoppe' where he went every morning to have his face shaved and his hair combed before he started work. There was no one around, so we explored all the different rooms and went inside the Oval Office. I asked where the President was and a member of staff told me he had retired to his upstairs suite for the night. He even showed me which window to look at to see if the lights were on.

Tom and his wife, Annette, would drive over to see us on special occasions, like my birthday, Christmas and for cookouts. They'd join us at Duxbury Beach where both our families would park their Jeeps. We also went on camping trips with them during the summer vacation. Dad bought a huge fold-up tent that came in a box and hitched to his Jeep. He'd pack sleeping bags, lanterns, coolers and camping equipment and create a mini home at campgrounds in New Hampshire or Massachusetts.

On one of these camping trips I got sick with high fever, chills and stomach ache. For the first time in my life, I prayed to God to help me to get well because I didn't want to go home. I prayed so hard. Then I felt the sun shining on me and suddenly I was fine, with no fever or any signs of illness. I couldn't believe it. I was about ten years old at the time. I said to myself, *Wow! God really does answer prayers.* So I always kept Him in the back of my mind in case of emergencies.

Chapter 3

I was enrolled at Chandler Elementary School in Duxbury, Massachusetts for the first year of kindergarten. As soon as I got off the bus I got lost because I couldn't hear the instructions over the loudspeakers or the teachers telling the children where to go. Eventually one of the teachers noticed I was upset. I told her I didn't know where to go in the best way I could speak. She was very nice and took me by the hand to my teacher, Mrs. Lindstrom.

Mrs. Lindstrom waved her hands and indicated to everyone to sit on the floor. Then she sat in a huge wooden rocking chair and held up a large book with a bear on the cover and started to tell the class a story. But because it was in front of her face I couldn't see her mouth to read her lips. While the other children were smiling and laughing I started to cry again. I was sobbing so hard the teacher called the resource aide who took me to another room and asked me what was wrong. The obvious thing to have done was to have told her I was deaf, but at that young age all I could do was cry.

The kids all stared at me because I had hearing aids strapped behind my ears. Then they began to point and whisper and make fun of me. When it was recess they'd run away and leave me standing on my own. I'd remain rooted to the spot covered in sand dust as they scattered across the playground.

This happened every day for weeks until one of my classmates, a black boy called James, who was also left on his own, smiled at me and said, "Let's go over there and play on the swings." We laughed as we swung higher and higher. Within a few minutes a crowd of kids surrounded us, chanting names, calling him nigger and calling me deaf and dumb, and ugly. I noticed poor James with his head down, so I found the courage to yell at them to stop in my struggled speech. Then James held my hand tightly and shouted at them to stop calling me deaf and ugly. The bell rang for the end of recess and we got in the line and went back inside. James looked at me with a huge smile and said, "You're my friend." We both hugged and continued to play together, ignoring the stares from the other children. James would motion to me where to go next in the playground. I'll never forget his kindness or the camaraderie we shared.

Meanwhile I was still struggling to understand my teacher. I couldn't read her lips because she stood so far away, so I read her facial expressions. I couldn't make sense of what she was writing on the chalk board either. The teacher's aide wrote notes for me but she didn't know sign language and the few words she wrote didn't give me the information I needed. It was embarrassing having someone sit with me. The other kids would snigger and give me funny looks.

When the teacher's aide was off sick I'd look around, wondering what to do. Sometimes I was told to read a book, but mostly I'd be told to sit at a triangular table facing the corner of the room and the teacher would forget I was there. I had no friends because I couldn't speak very well. This went on until I was in third grade. By then my speech had improved, thanks to hours of therapy, but it was still far from normal.

Thank goodness for the arrival of closed caption TV. My dad came into the living room and hooked up the closed captions box, read the instructions and got it up and running. It only worked on a few series, such as *The Disney Show*, *The Waltons* and *Little House on the Prairie*. I'd watch these shows for hours, trying to understand what the words meant.

Things at school were still bad. Every day I'd return home and cry on the couch. My mother would try to comfort me and encourage me not to give up. I'd say, "Why can't the other kids accept me? Why can't they be my friends? I just don't understand." I was convinced it was because I was too ugly. I wished I had blond hair and blue eyes like a fairytale princess instead of being dark haired and brown eyed with hearing aids and big black glasses. All I dreamed about was being pretty and popular.

At the beginning of fourth grade everyone was required to play the violin as part of a program to teach extracurricular activities. The teacher told us how to position it on our shoulder and how to hold the bow. But I couldn't hear the notes and didn't understand what she was saying. I only got one part right, which was how to hold the violin. While the teacher was out of the room, the kids gathered around me and chanted, "You're deaf!" "You're dumb!" "You're ugly!" The tears poured from my eyes as I stood there feeling so humiliated. They challenged me to play my instrument and laughed because I had no idea. This went on for several weeks. When I told my mom what was happening she said I just had to go along with it.

Then one day, during violin class, I lost my temper and screamed at the teacher that I was deaf and couldn't do it. I threw the violin on the floor. The teacher was so angry she grabbed me by my shirt and dragged me out of the classroom to the principal's office. The principal called my mother and said I had damaged an expensive piece of school property and would be suspended for three days.

My father argued that I was deaf and they had no right to force me to play the violin. So they let me go to the library to help put the books away once a week instead. Unfortunately, I couldn't understand the librarian because she had an accent and talked very softly, so I didn't know how to put books back in the right order. I was afraid to ask her to explain everything again in case she made me go back to the violin class. So I just put the books back randomly when no one was watching. At the end of the school year, the librarians had to take all the books off the shelves and start over because they thought so many titles were missing or stolen. I saw them through the window, reorganizing everything, on my way to speech therapy. *Oh boy*, I thought to myself.

Chapter 4

When I was about eight, my dad took out his old film projector to play some old family movies on a pull-out screen in our basement. Everyone had their homemade buttered popcorn and plopped down onto the orange couch. Dad said, "Are you ready?"

"Yes!" we all shouted excitedly.

I saw myself on a beach talking to my brother. I stared at this girl and thought how weird she looked. Her mouth was open wide and when she talked her tongue was sticking out and she was making strange faces. All the movies were the same. There I was, exaggerating every word and looking ridiculous. I was so embarrassed I ran upstairs. Everyone shouted, "Hey where are you going?"

I told them, "I'm leaving because I hate myself!" I sat in front of the mirror of the dressing table in my walk-in closet and studied myself as I spoke. Never again was I going to look like I did in those family movies. I practiced for hours every day until I was able to keep my tongue inside my mouth and look normal. After school I'd say the same word over and over, modifying my facial movements until I was able to control my mouth like a hearing person. I even moved my small black-and-white TV closer to my bed so I could study the actors' faces better and copy them perfectly. While I was watching TV I would hold my pink plastic-framed mirror and mimic their expressions. I was determined to get it right.

Before long I could go into stores and the cashier would say something and I'd say, "Can you please repeat that because I am deaf?"

The cashier would reply, "Oh wow, I had no idea. You don't look like a deaf person."

In fifth grade I made friends with a girl called Nicole. I called her Nikki. We clicked right away. If I asked her to say something again she'd repeat it to me patiently. She lived a couple of streets away from me and we'd go to each other's houses at the weekends. Nikki introduced me to her friends and included me in activities such as ice skating, roller skating and sledding. At recess I'd play on the monkey bars with her and her friend Heather, or we'd get chased around the playground by the boys. Finally, I felt part of the normal hearing world.

One day Nikki and Heather came up to me in the playground. I could tell right away there was something wrong. Heather said, "Just tell her. Get it over with and do it out loud so she can hear."

Nikki turned to me with tears in her eyes and said, "I'm so sorry. I can't invite you to my birthday party."

"What? I thought we were best friends?" I said.

She told me they were going to the Boston Aquarium to look at fish and her mom didn't want a deaf person there because I'd be too much trouble and wouldn't understand what the tour guide was saying.

"Can't I just look at the fish and the sea animals? I won't complain. I promise. Please?" I begged.

Heather said, "Haven't you noticed that none of the girls in your class invited you to their birthday parties? They didn't want you there because you're deaf and ugly."

I ran away to the far side of the playground and sat down in the sand. I felt as if my heart had been ripped out of my chest. It was true. I hadn't been invited to a single party during all of my elementary school years but I'd never realized it until she mentioned it. I burst into huge sobs. Then I ran even further to the edge of the school grounds where I could cry alone. I didn't want to live anymore. All I wanted was to have friends like everyone else. It wasn't fair that I couldn't hear. Didn't anyone understand that being deaf wasn't my fault? The bell rang and the kids went inside. I stayed where I was until a teacher's aide found me and tried to drag me to my feet. Eventually I got up and made my way towards the school building and was sent to the nurse's office to calm down.

Yet again I went home crying on the bus and then sobbed into the couch in the family room. My mother tried to comfort me by telling me I could have my own birthday party. That just made me mad. "Don't you understand?" I screamed. "No one wants to be my friend because I'm deaf and ugly!"

I was eleven in May and I invited everyone to my slumber birthday party, including Nikki and Heather. Nikki's mom wouldn't let her stay overnight and she was only allowed to stay a few hours. She showed up late while I was opening my presents on the deck outside. Everyone had made an effort to dress nicely, but she was still in her jeans and T-shirt. She had red eyes like she'd been crying. I felt sad for her because I knew it wasn't her fault she had to leave early.

The celebration was going well and everyone was having a good time until night time came. We all had our pajamas on and were getting ready to go to sleep when all of sudden someone pulled down my pajama pants with my underwear inside. I quickly pulled everything up and then I watched in dismay as my so-called friends rolled about laughing and pointing at me calling me ugly.

I didn't want to stay downstairs with them, so I went upstairs crying and slept in my bedroom alone. I was mortified that they had seen my naked privates. I couldn't believe they would humiliate me like that at my own party. My mother tried to get me to go back downstairs and join them. That was the end of my birthday sleepover. I never did it again for years.

The next day my parents took me to Duxbury's annual festival. They tried so hard to cheer me up by buying me candy apples and popcorn but there was nothing they could do to make things better. I was overwhelmed with misery and it showed on my face and in my silence.

Crying became my new normal. There was hardly a moment when my cheeks weren't wet or tear-stained. I'd cry when I went to school and cry getting off the bus. Then I'd go to my sad couch and weep some more. I tried to explain to my mother how much I hated school but all she did was give me candy and tell me I could watch TV instead of doing chores. Then she would repeat the same unhelpful advice. "Just ignore them," and "Don't pay attention to them." She didn't report the matter or confront the kids who were making my life hell. I just had to deal with it.

Chapter 5

Our house was decorated in country style with chintzy flower prints, beige rugs and dark wooden furniture. The wood-paneled walls were hung with dried flower displays. I especially loved my pink bedroom with its wooden four-poster bed and white canopy. I had dark-brown Ethan Allen furniture, with shelves for books and a desk where I did my homework. Inside my spacious walk-in closet there was a blue painted vanity with a huge mirror. It gave me so much pleasure spending time in there playing with make-up and fixing my hair. But it wasn't long before those cruel words from school would enter my head: "You're deaf, you're dumb … you're so ugly!"

Maybe it was possible for me to fix the situation and alter my face with make-up? Perhaps if I looked pretty they wouldn't go after me again? So I experimented with eyeliner, mascara and eyeshadows from the age of ten. I told my parents I needed to make myself look better. They felt sorry for me so they let me have my way despite my young age.

I got hooked on make-up and loved how it transformed my appearance. Everyone in my family told me I was a beautiful girl but I had a hard time believing them due to the constant barrage of abuse at school: "You're too tall ... your feet are too big ... your glasses are ugly ..."

Across the street from us, there were six children in the McCrans family. I envied them because their mom was so cool. She would talk to them on a bench swing outside their house. My mother was the exact opposite. She would scream at me when my brother and I got into a fight or started bickering and spank us with a wooden spoon or a stick. Being punished like that didn't teach me anything but resentment and made my heart grow cold towards her.

I wanted Mrs. McCran to adopt me because then she would sit and listen to the things that were bothering me. I bet she would have taken action to help me, rather than just brushing me off. At one of my low points I went over to her house and said, "Is it alright if I tell you about my problems?"

"Sure," she replied. We sat on her talking bench and I told her I wasn't happy in school because I didn't understand a word anyone was saying. She looked at me with tears in her eyes and said, "Maybe you can ask your parents to find another school where you feel like you belong; one that makes you happy."

I'd never thought of that before and kept the idea in the back of my mind. A few weeks later I saw a 'House for Sale' sign in her front yard. When I learned they were moving to California I was devastated. They moved away and my dream family was replaced with a smaller one with two little boys.

Every Sunday the newspaper would arrive and I'd turn to the cartoons, the 'Dear Abby' problem page and 'Sunday's Child', which featured children that needed adopting, with a picture of the kid and their details underneath. One weekend I saw a girl who was deaf and exactly like me, the same age and everything. She would be the perfect sister for me. I rushed to my parents, who were sitting at the breakfast table, and said, "Look! Can we adopt her, please? Please?"

They glanced at the paper and immediately said no. I pleaded, "Why? We have plenty of room in this house and I need a deaf sister who can understand how I feel, then I won't be the only one in school and my family being deaf."

My mother rolled her eyes and sighed, "Jeez Jen, we can't save the world. The answer is no."

I cut out the girl's picture and stuck it to my wall and daydreamed about how wonderful it would be for me to have a deaf sister. I kept asking my parents if they would call the number and begged them for weeks. Finally my mom got mad at me and yelled, "No, and if you bring this up one more time I'm going to take away your TV time and you can do extra chores as a punishment."

Then she told me the deaf girl had probably been adopted already. I realized my dream was gone. At that moment I vowed that when I had children, I'd make sure they had brothers and sisters to play with.

Chapter 6

I entered Duxbury Middle School as a sixth grader. It wasn't structured like the elementary school and I had an anxiety attack as soon as I stepped off the bus. All the kids looked so much bigger and were wearing much cooler clothes. I recognized a few of them from my old school. I waved at them but they didn't wave back because they didn't want to be associated with the weird girl who couldn't hear.

Having no idea of where I was supposed to go, I followed the signs to the principal's office and told the lady at the reception desk that I was lost. "Didn't you hear the announcements over the loudspeakers?" she asked. I explained to her that I didn't because I was deaf. She looked irritated. "Wait here," she instructed, "I'll call someone to show you where to go." Half an hour later the bell rang and I was still waiting for help. Finally, an eighth grader asked me for my schedule. I handed it to her and she took me down the corridors and showed me where everything was. I paid close attention so I didn't miss anything.

I showed up a little late for my first English class and walked in during the lesson. Everyone looked me up and down. I noticed that all the girls were wearing better clothes than me, with high-heeled pumps. I didn't own any fashionable shoes or even a piece of jewelry. My parents didn't believe in wasting money on frivolities because they were saving all their money for their retirement.

One very attractive girl with highlighted hair, wearing a pale-pink cashmere sweater and pearls, looked at me and said, "Wow, you're so plain, and what are you wearing? Jeez!" She pointed to my chunky flat sneakers with a horrified look. I wanted to run away and hide. Instead, I sat as far to the back of the classroom as possible so there was no one behind me to point and make jokes.

It got harder for me to learn because a teacher's aide would only show up once in a while. Then I'd tell her to leave because I was ashamed of being deaf and wanted to look like a hearing person. Lunch time was also a challenge. I'd go to an empty table, hoping someone would join me, but usually nobody did.

I hardly saw my old best friend Nikki. Occasionally I'd see her standing by her locker and she'd give me a half smile as I passed her in the hallway. Her friends would bully me mercilessly when she wasn't looking. They'd walk past me using fake sign language, making rude gestures, pulling faces and mocking the way I tried to speak.

A few other girls who weren't a part of the mean girl crowd approached me. Their names were Heather, Debbie and Robin. I suspect they did it partly out of pity as they always saw me standing on my own. We started to talk and discovered we had a lot of the same classes together. These girls were troublemakers and not respectful to the teachers. But I didn't care. All that mattered was that they wanted to be my friends, so I invited them over to my house.

We were all hanging out in my garage, which was full of boxes of leftover stuff from a yard sale we'd had over the weekend. My mother was planning to drop them off at the charity store the next day. They decided to open up some boxes for a bit of fun. Debbie and Heather found a couple of long flower-print skirts that I didn't want anymore and said they loved them. I told them they could have them since they were mine and they were going to charity.

Suddenly my mother opened the garage door and asked what we were doing. I told her I was giving my skirts to Debbie and Heather. She got angry and told them to put them back in the box. I was shocked and embarrassed, and my friends stood there in disbelief. I calmly told my mother it was okay because they were mine and I was letting them have them. Despite my explanation my mother said, "No!" flatly, then in a loud voice she commanded, "Please put those things back now. Your friends can't have them."

They quickly put everything back without saying a word. When she was gone they said, "Wow, your mother is really mean. We don't feel welcome here, we're leaving." I was so hurt because I wanted so badly to have friends to hang out with. They never came back to my house again. It soon got round the school about how rude and nasty my mother was and being my friend was no fun.

Chapter 7

One morning, as I went to my usual place at the back of the classroom for English, I saw a black girl had decided to go there too. We looked at each other and smiled. Then we exchanged notes and learned each other's names. I told her I didn't understand what the lesson was about and she wrote that she would tell me what the teacher was saying. We compared our schedules and found out we had many classes together. I was so excited. I'd found a new friend who was willing to hang out with me and sit with me in the cafeteria. Her name was Tracey Washington.

I never found her again after I left Duxbury High School, although I have searched everywhere for her. All I remember is that she moved to Washington D.C. to live with her aunt when her grandmother passed away from cancer.

At break time Tracey told me to follow her outside to the back of the cafeteria where a few of the students went to smoke. She pulled out a pack of Marlboro Lights and a plastic lighter and asked if I wanted to join her. It was the first time I had ever touched a cigarette. I tried to inhale but immediately choked on the bitter smoke. Everyone laughed because I was coughing so much. Tracey told me to keep her cigarettes and practice. So I'd sneak out to the woods and force myself to draw the smoke into my lungs. Then I'd brush my teeth and spray myself with perfume so my parents wouldn't suspect anything. I soon became an expert smoker like Tracey.

One warm summer's day, a tall, handsome boy with long feathered back hair joined us behind the cafeteria. His name was Craig. He wore a flashy black leather biker jacket and jeans because he came to school on a motorcycle ridden by his friend Larry. Larry was a senior and very popular with the girls. I tried to talk to Craig in my own awkward way but he didn't want anything to do with me. These two cool boys didn't notice that I was making an effort to get to know them, but the other boys did. One of them was a senior, over six feet tall with blond hair. He asked me if I wanted to escape with him to the woods behind the school. I thought, *Wow, that's a cool idea! I always wanted to escape from school.* I didn't realize he was going to try to have sex with me.

We sat down on the yellow grass and he leaned over and pressed his mouth against mine. It was my first ever proper kiss. He kept trying to put his hand inside my pants and I knocked his arm away and told him, "No!" but he insisted on touching me. Finally, I kicked him in the groin. He got very angry and said we had to go back to class. We walked back together and that was the last time I ever saw him. But it wasn't the end of the matter, because he told everyone that I'd had sex with him in the woods.

Students looked at me in horror and giggled wherever I went. I'd sit at a table in the cafeteria and people would get up and move to another one. In class I'd find notes on my desk calling me a slut. Someone even stuck a picture of a naked woman on my chair with my name written over it.

I dreamt about getting a gun and shooting everyone in the cafeteria. I obsessed about getting hold of an automatic rifle so I could slaughter as many people as possible and then kill myself before the police arrived. One weekend we went to my Gram and Uncle Pete's house. Uncle Pete had lots of guns but they were all kept locked up in a glass cabinet. I desperately wanted to grab one of the guns and some boxes of bullets and take them home. I sat for hours in the living room waiting to see if Uncle Pete would open his gun closet and forget to lock it. It never happened. I was so disappointed.

Today I look back and think thank goodness he kept it secured because I didn't know what I was doing. If that gun cabinet had been left open I would probably not be here today. I would either be dead or jailed for life. It does make me understand, though, why kids that are alienated and bullied feel they have nothing to live for and go on shooting rampages.

Chapter 8

With my new reputation as a whore on top of being called ugly, dumb and deaf, I was glad I knew how to smoke because it took away some of the stress. Hanging out with the smokers in their jean jackets became the highlight of my day. I'd go outside in freezing temperatures and pouring rain. I only understood about thirty percent of the conversation and just copied everyone's facial expressions. I never asked anyone to repeat anything because I wanted to look like a hearing person.

The smoking group all wore jeans or leather skirts and had red or blue bandannas tied around their necks or heads. They seemed to be gang members and I later learned that they were known as the 'druggie crowd.' They looked at my Kmart jeans and plain shirt and laughed, and said I needed to change my image if I wanted to hang with them.

I begged my mom to buy me some new outfits, so she took me to the mall and I picked out a Levi's jean jacket, a couple of bandannas, a black leather mini skirt, some little tops and some shirts. I got rid of all my pastel-colored, girly clothes and mainly wore black. My parents were confused by my sudden transformation. I got defensive and told them I had to fit in with my new set of friends. They didn't say a word. They knew that I had cried almost every day after school and if this made me happy then it was a good thing.

The next morning I wore a dark-purple sleeveless top, with a red bandanna around my neck, and black mini skirt with black leather boots. I added more make-up and eyeliner than usual and went downstairs. My mother looked at me in a shock, saying, "I don't think you should dress up like that. Go upstairs and change." I adamantly refused. When I got to school I felt everyone's eyes on me. I had also taken my glasses off and put them in my school bag, which made a huge difference. My old friends from elementary school were like, "What happened to you overnight? You look really good."

I felt so much more confident with my new cool image and was invited to go out with the smoking group. We'd go roller-skating on Friday nights, have sleepovers and hang out at the mall. My new image even gave me the courage to confront anyone who called me names. I'd grab their hair or punch them if they dared to mock me.

Going home on the bus one day I saw a boy who'd been calling me ugly and deaf for months. I went up to him, pulled his book bag off his back and dumped its contents on the floor while the bus was moving. He was supposed to get off at the next stop but he was too busy picking up his books, which were sliding under the seats. I threw some of them out the bus window at him when he got off.

The following week I got into another fight with a girl who had taken my hairbrush from my bag and wouldn't give it back. She was waving it in the air and the whole class thought it was hilarious. Something inside of me exploded. I grabbed her by the waist and threw her across the room over a desk. She crashed up against the bookshelves and the room fell into a shocked silence. Then the teacher came in, assessed the scene and sent us both to the principal's office. My parents were told to come and pick me up. I was suspended for four days and missed the school dance.

My dad was sympathetic and understood that I had been bullied. To cheer me up he took us all out to my favorite steak restaurant on the day of the dance and bought me shoes, jewelry and make-up at the mall. We finished up the evening with quarter pounders with cheese and French fries from McDonalds. My dad always told me that people didn't understand that I was deaf, because I spoke so well. But of course it didn't mean I could hear and that was a huge problem. Back in the 1980s there was no education about bullying. There were no anti-bullying policies or anti-bigotry programs. Nothing was done to help people like me.

That same year, my parents thought I would benefit from being enrolled in a modeling agency's summer school to boost my self-confidence. I told them I wasn't pretty enough but they convinced me to give it a chance.

I fell in love with modeling school because it taught me how to apply make-up professionally and how to choose the right clothes. I also learned how to pose for photos. One photo shoot took place at 4am at the beach. I picked out an aqua-colored button-down shirt and a long, white ruffled skirt and walked through the waves, and wore a bathing suit for other shots.

I went to this school all summer and really thought it would lead to paid modeling work for magazines and TV commercials. But this was not the case, as I would discover. At the end of the course we were called to see the modeling agency's director. I saw one girl running out of her office crying. What was going on? Then another girl, who was very beautiful, came out smiling. When it was my turn I felt like the director had my life in her hands as she went through my photos. She told me I was a very striking girl but I needed rhinoplasty to make my nose smaller and I wasn't cute enough for TV commercials.

I burst into tears. I had made a fool out of myself and was stupid for ever thinking I could be a model. But she did go on to say that I had attractive hands and maybe I could be a hand model. I told her to forget it. That was not my idea of modeling. It was a crushing blow to hear that I had a big nose. I had never thought my nose was big until she pointed it out. I realized the kids who had made fun of me were right. I was ugly.

Chapter 9

I hated chemistry class because the teacher looked like a German Nazi with his clipped hair and small head. He'd talk and write on the board so fast that I couldn't make out anything he said to the class. I copied my friend Tracey's test papers but unfortunately she was no good at chemistry either. All of my tests and homework were graded 'F.'

As I was now in tenth grade, it was my responsibility to go to the resource room and ask Mr. Williamson and another assistant for help. They were on hand to cater for the three other deaf students in the school. I stopped by and I saw a red-haired girl named Susan sitting at the table. The resource aide teacher was doing her homework for her and even her written test. I couldn't believe it. That girl wasn't going to learn anything! Years later I found out that Susan got a job as a maid in a motel.

I decided to give Mr. Williamson one shot to help me with my homework. Just as he had done with Susan, he gave me the answers instead of explaining things to me. He was cheating me and cheating the school. That was my last attempt at asking for help. Instead I spent hours in the library trying to figure things out. I didn't want to end up making beds for a living.

My dad had graduated from Northeastern University in Boston and his awards and degrees were all displayed in his office. He was also on the college football team, which was the first in the school's history to remain undefeated. My mother graduated from Fisher Junior College as a secretary. She mastered shorthand and I thought it was cool that she knew all these secret writing codes.

I knew in my heart that education was important and I wanted to be successful. But I was scared because there didn't seem to be any point in being at Duxbury High School. I wasn't acquiring any skills except how to kill time and smoke cigarettes. Some days I'd hide in a bathroom stall and watch the girls do their hair and make-up through the crack of the door. I'd write things on the stall walls or just sit there with my head in my hands waiting for the bell to sound. Then I'd go home and sit in front of my mirror inside my walk-in closet trying to figure out how to act like a hearing person or I would try out new hairstyles and new ways of using make-up. I spent so long correcting my outward appearance and then hiding from people because I was paranoid that I still looked ugly.

The only class I liked was art because it was practical and easy to comprehend. The teacher demonstrated everything and would give us all the same materials. I was good at water color painting and line drawing. But I knew art wasn't a serious subject, so I decided to join the girls' field hockey team and to write poems for the Duxbury High School newsletter club. I wanted to be a part of mainstream school activities and not just the rebel crowd. I dreamed of making my parents proud and if I became a jock like the other girls, maybe they'd be impressed. The hockey team wore white shorts and dark-green Duxbury shirts with white numbers. I wasn't good enough to play in the match so I was on the bench a lot. The coach would only let me play in the last quarter when the game was almost over, or if they were winning by a big margin.

One day at practice, I noticed a group of girls and boys sitting down on the grass pointing at me and laughing at me. I couldn't figure out what was so funny. I was practicing shooting balls and was bending over a lot because I'm tall and the hockey stick only reached my knees. I went to the bathroom in the toilet block behind the field to make sure there was nothing on my face or grass stains on my clothes. When I pulled down my shorts and underwear I was shocked to see they were soaked in bright-red blood. It was my first menstrual period. I had no pads or tampons on me and I didn't know what to do because the school was closed for the day. I couldn't go back out to the field to face those girls and their jock boyfriends. There was no way I was going to ask any of them for help. So I wrapped my jacket around my waist and started to walk home. It was a journey that took half an hour on the bus so I knew I'd be walking for hours. I made my way back in tears, planning how to kill myself.

I desperately wanted to shoot everyone in the school cafeteria. I had to get hold of a gun. Maybe I could ask for shooting lessons and convince my parents to buy me a pistol to practice with. Or maybe I could ask my uncle to let me use one of his guns and then tell him I wanted a rifle for my birthday. Or I could get an older boy at school to get hold of one for me. Then I thought how devastated my dad would be if I was gone.

A car pulled over and a man rolled the window down and said, "Do you need a ride? You're a long way from Duxbury High."

He had obviously noticed my uniform. I said, "Okay," and sat down on my jacket and a book from my backpack so I wouldn't bleed on his seats. I showed him where my home was. I didn't care if he tried to kill me because I wanted to die anyway. But he didn't do anything and kindly dropped me off at the end of my street. I ran up to the front door and unlocked it with the key from under the doormat. Then I found my mother's self-adhesive pads in one of her dresser drawers. After I had showered I stuck one inside my underwear and prepared to tell my parents that I was never going back to that school.

When she got home from work I told my mother what had happened. As usual she said, "Never mind, don't worry about it." She forced me to go to school the next day armed with sanitary pads in my book bag. The whole school knew what had happened. Everyone giggled at me in the hallway and one boy threw a piece of red paper at me. Some girls from the hockey team fell about laughing hysterically. Again I wished I owned a gun to shoot them all.

The next day I went to the smoking area as usual. Everyone had gathered in a group to follow a tall, skinny foreign-looking man to the gym because he needed to talk to us. Unfortunately he had a mustache so I couldn't make out what he was saying. Some girls were crying on each other's shoulders. I imagined that someone had gotten into trouble and they were upset because they didn't like the rules.

When he had finished, the man told everyone to go back to their classrooms, then he walked up behind me and said, "I want to talk to you privately." I tried to decipher the words coming out of his mouth but it was hard to read his lips, so I had to rely on my hearing aids. He asked, "Do you know what we talked about?" I replied that I didn't. Then he explained, slowly and seriously, "Your friend Craig was killed in motorcycle accident yesterday."

That handsome Craig who I had always secretly admired was on the back of Larry's motorcycle when they were hit by a car. Larry was in the hospital with a broken leg but Craig was killed instantly. I screamed inside and felt so mad that I was deaf and didn't know what had happened when everyone else did. I'd had a crush on Craig for the past two years. I couldn't believe he was dead.

His funeral was held a few days later. Of course, I didn't know what anyone was saying but I could read their faces. It was so sad to see his little brother who looked just like him with his hair feathered back. He was holding Craig's black leather jacket and looked so forlorn sitting on the front pew. His parents were sobbing, with tissue boxes on their laps. It was a heart-wrenching sight. Then Larry hobbled to his seat on crutches. His leg was in a fresh white cast as a contrast to all the black that people were wearing. He took his seat and didn't look up the entire time. I felt so bad for Larry because he would remember this tragedy for rest of his life.

There was a huge gold-framed picture of Craig next to a closed coffin. They didn't have an open casket because his face had been badly smashed-up in the accident. He was so good looking, standing in the middle of a circle of girls, smoking in the courtyard. He had such a magnetic personality and danced like John Travolta in his white suit and black shirt.

After this cruel lesson I did a lot of thinking and realized I was lucky to be alive. Craig's life had been cut short. He would never graduate, never go to college, never get married, have children or even a future. That was all gone.

Chapter 10

My classes and everything outside of them were getting worse and harder. I had no clue what my homework was about or what I was supposed to be learning. I didn't want the resource teacher aide to give me the answers, so I asked Susan, the deaf girl who was two years ahead of me, how she managed. Susan didn't know how to talk like me and was totally deaf, with no hearing aids. It was like talking to a first-grader. I realized people assumed we were on the same level, which is why they called me dumb.

A cloud of darkness swallowed me up and I felt the strongest urge to end my life. I was exhausted. I was tired of being clueless in class and fed up with the random bullying that came at me out of nowhere every day. I remembered Mrs. McCran and her suggestion about going to another school.

I went to chemistry class and was handed my test result. There was a huge red letter 'F' on the first page. I couldn't survive another two years at Duxbury High School. There were only two options that I could see. I could shoot all my classmates and kill myself or leave forever. I walked out of the class and trekked down the long hallway. None of the staff tried to stop me from leaving. I was done. One by one I threw the books from my locker across the hallway, creating a mess of torn pages and broken spines. Then I put the things I wanted in my school bag, went downstairs to reception and walked through the big double doors for the last time.

I kept on walking, looking straight ahead, with tears running down my face. I knew it would be a very long journey by foot. This time I got no ride home and it took me more than two hours to reach my front door. I got inside, put the TV on and sat and stared at it blankly. A few hours later, my brother Antonio came home and asked me what was wrong. I told him I'd quit school and he laughed and said, "Yeah right!"

Then I sat on the dark-orange recliner and waited for the dreaded moment my parents returned home from work. I knew by now they must have received a phone call, since all the broken books in the hallway had my name on them. Sure enough, they both came home early. The principal had informed them that I hadn't attended any of my classes that day except for two and I had deliberately destroyed school property.

I looked at them directly and announced, "I've quit high school. You have to find me a school where I can understand using sign language. I know I have told you not to sign to me because I am ashamed of being deaf, but I've changed my mind. It's better for me. I will never go back to Duxbury ever again."

"Oh, you will go back there tomorrow and you'll be fine," my mom replied, ignoring my request as if she'd never heard me.

"No!" I repeated angrily. "No way am I going back there." Then I screamed at them, "My answer is final and you can't make me go!"

The next morning my mother tried to wake me up to go to school. Once again I told her I was staying home. Then my father came in and dragged me out of bed, telling me I was going even if it meant I'd be wearing my pajamas. I was so mad at him and shouted, "You can't make me go! I am not going back. Find me another school! I can't understand anything! I'm not learning anything! Stop pretending I can hear!"

I sat at home watching TV for three weeks in the orange recliner until my parents told me they had found a place called Boston School for the Deaf, which mainstreamed at Randolph High School. It was about an hour's drive away with traffic, so I would have to live in the girls' dormitory. Dad's work was fifteen minutes away from the school, so he took me to meet the administrative staff. I wore normal clothes: plain black pants and a pink plaid shirt. I wanted to start afresh. As well as dressing more conservatively, I told myself I was no longer going to smoke.

The school was in a huge old red-brick building at the top of a hill and was run by Catholic nuns as well as qualified teachers. As I was being shown around I noticed everyone was signing and mouthing words and laughing. It was so silly of me not to allow my parents to sign. All I knew was a few basic signs and the letters of the alphabet. How ironic that now I couldn't even have a conversation with a deaf person!

I followed the administrator to a small building to do some tests. Then they discussed my placement and their routines. Four boys around my age looked at me and smiled. While my dad and the officials were talking, I waited in the administrator's office.

Knowing the boys were watching my every move I sat at the desk with my legs crossed and my hands behind my head looking up to the ceiling, pretending I was a model. One of the boys looked to be Egyptian or from somewhere in the Middle East. He peeked through the door and I waved to him. He waved back and then stumbled backwards. I laughed and he quickly got up and ran away with his pals. Then an official came into the office with my father and told me that I had scored so high on the tests that I didn't qualify to go to any of the deaf-only classes.

"What? That's not fair! It's my dream to be with other deaf kids. Why can't I just try it? Please!" I said, hardly believing what I was being told. The school taught students to speak and sign simultaneously, which was something I had to learn. The official explained that I would attend homeroom at the deaf school and then take a bus to Randolph High School at the other side of town to attend mainstream classes with sign language interpreters. There would be other deaf kids there and I shouldn't worry about it.

I begged him to let me experience just one week of deaf student-only classes, saying I would let him know if I found the lessons too easy or too hard. If they were too easy I would go to the other high school. He thought about it, shook my hand and said, "Deal."

Next, I was introduced to a staff member called Mrs. White who took me over to the girls' dormitory to show me my room. We walked for what seemed like miles, through lots of heavy, glass swinging doors and down corridors with marble floors and antique wooden doors along their walls. The nuns were dressed in black-and-white habits and I kept staring at them, wondering how they could wear such heavy robes and cover their heads every day. It must be so uncomfortable and hot. On the way upstairs to the dormitory, I noticed an enormous living room with couches and a TV, with closed captioning, on a stand in the corner. A heavy, oak door led to each dormitory room. Each room had two twin beds except for one at the end of the hallway, which had a full-sized bed. That was a private room and was a special privilege that could be earned by a senior who got good grades.

My parents had to collect all the paperwork from my old school and transfer it to my new one, which delayed my move by a few days. So I agreed to go back to Duxbury High School for the last two days of the week. I didn't want anyone to know that I was leaving and wanted to go quietly without any fuss. But I wanted to leave them with one final message. So I submitted one of my glamorous black-and-white modeling photos and a poem entitled *Silent World* to the school newsletter. I met with the science teacher, who was editing this quarterly publication, and handed him an envelope with my poem and photo inside. He pulled out the contents, raised his eyebrows, quickly read the poem and said, "Wow, this is a wonderful piece of writing and your photo is beautiful."

On my last day I was in biology when someone from the office came into the classroom and whispered in the teacher's ear. The teacher pointed at me and announced to the class that I was leaving. I was so mad because didn't want anyone to know. Everyone turned and gazed at me, their mouths open in a shock.

Why should they care? All they had done was make fun of me, embarrass me and put me through hell.

News of my departure spread like wildfire down the hallways. I didn't want their insincere hugs or goodbyes because none of them had ever treated me with kindness or respect. I didn't need to worry, as none of them said a word to me.

Chapter 11

I was thrilled to be starting a whole new chapter of my new life and wanted to make sure I made a great first impression. Mom went with me to the mall and bought some new clothes and a twin-sized comforter and sheets. My parents had never seen me so happy.

Monday arrived quickly. My father put my brand-new bright-pink suitcase on wheels into the trunk and dropped me off at school on his way to work. He lectured me in the car about following the rules and behaving respectfully to the teachers. Then he gave me a big hug, kissed my cheek and wished me luck.

I met with the supervisor again and she put my suitcase in a closet, locked the door and said I could unpack after school had finished. Next she led me to my homeroom and explained that this was where everyone did their homework and watched TV. I noticed all the deaf kids tracking me with their eyes as I walked by. I was thrilled to see the Egyptian boy was among them. Everyone was signing so fast in the air. I didn't know what they were saying because their fingers were moving so quickly. A wave of fear hit me. Was I going to be bullied because I didn't know sign language that well? Please God, please don't let it happen again.

The foreign-looking boy I liked was called David and his buddies were Tim and Joseph. The girls were called Kathy, who looked like a mini version of me, Jackie, who was very short, and a few others whose names I can't recall. I thought, *Wow! There are only twelve kids in here.* I was in for culture shock. There were around thirty-five students in my old homeroom at Duxbury High and I still didn't have any friends. Here there were just a dozen kids. What if they all decided to gang up against me?

David smiled and signed something, but I didn't understand his message. I looked to Kathy for help and she finger spelled what he was saying. Then I put my hand up near my mouth and finger spelled to Kathy that I thought David was cute. She thought it was so funny that I covered my face for privacy. I later found out that in the deaf community you have to turn your back or go in another room if you don't want someone to know what you are thinking. I had no clue about deaf mannerisms and etiquette.

I understood the homeroom teacher because she signed and used her voice at the same time. It was the first time in my life I understood my teacher! The bell rang to indicate that everyone had to clear out of homeroom and go to their classes or take the bus to Randolph High. I stayed behind to attend the deaf English class with David, Kathy, Joseph, Tim and Jackie. The English teacher also used a combination of voice and signing. I soon realized that I already knew everything and this was like a third-grade lesson to me. I got an easy 'A' in that class. I kept looking over at David because I had a huge crush on him already. I thought he was so handsome, with his dark eyes, olive skin and big Egyptian nose, and he was tall like me.

The bell rang, which meant we had to take the bus to Randolph High, a few blocks away. A rattling old vehicle pulled up. It looked like a retired prison bus that had been painted dark blue to match the school's colors. A herd of students piled in from all different grades, from freshman to senior. I was relieved to see more new faces. One girl ran up to me signing fast and speaking excitedly at the same time. She asked if I would join the girls' basketball team as I was so tall at five feet ten inches. I told her that it wasn't something that interested me. I didn't like the idea of running up and down and sweating unnecessarily. She kept on begging me so I told her I'd think about it.

Then another girl came up to me and said hello. She was dressed up in a punk fashion and wore lots of dark make up and some long silver Goth style earrings. She signed and tried to speak to me simultaneously because she knew I wasn't an expert signer. I loved her appearance and immediately wanted to form a bond with this girl. She looked like a kindred spirit to me. She said her name was Cathy D. I said, "Nice to meet you! I can't wait to be friends." Then she started to laugh along with some other girls and gave me a funny look. "Here we go again," I thought, "the outsider looking in." I was so worried I wouldn't be liked by these girls and was dreading the thought of being subjected to the same awful treatment I'd endured at Duxbury High.

After a bone-jangling ride we arrived at Randolph High. It was a massive campus, far bigger than Duxbury High. I noticed the kids were wearing a wide range of clothes. There were jeans, plaid shirts, T-shirts, tank tops and lots of unique garments, accessories and jewelry. At Duxbury the kids mostly wore polo shirts and high heels. I was relieved that I didn't see a single girl wearing fancy pumps or pearl necklaces. They mostly wore flats, sneakers, Vans and clogs.

David gestured to me to follow him to class. Unfortunately he wasn't on the same schedule as me. Then I saw a lady sitting in a chair opposite an empty seat and table. She waved to me and indicated that I should sit down in front of her. I was thinking, *Oh no! I never sit in the front row.* My place was at the back of the classroom out of sight and out of mind. My face flushed hot because everyone's attention was on me. I was in a panic sitting up there in front of everyone with everyone staring into the back of my head. The teacher started to speak very fast and the lady sitting across from me interpreted everything she said in real time using sign language. I was in a shock. For the first time I understood the entire class!

After a long day, the regular yellow buses arrived for hearing students, while the deaf kids lined up separately to wait for their decrepit blue bus. I sat with Kathy and Joseph because I felt safe with them. Kathy would laugh with me because I would try to make jokes using facial expressions. I finger spelled a lot but I had learned some new signs from the interpreter. David came up and sat in the seat across from me and asked me if I was going to the Valentine's dance on Thursday night. I replied, "Yes, I'm going and I can't wait!"

The supervisor was waiting for me when I got off the bus. She wanted to introduce me to Jane, the girls' dorm supervisor. She was a heavyset chatty woman. She told me how much I was going to love it there and showed me to my room. Then she told me my roommate was called Bridgette Ford. I laughed and said her name reminded me of the car manufacturer. When Jane told me she was descended from the Ford family I was taken aback and said, "Wow! That's crazy!"

A small skinny girl with short mousy hair quietly entered the room. She introduced herself as Bridgette and spelled out her name. I felt kind of disappointed because I wanted to have a roommate who loved make-up and clothes. Jane told me that Bridgette would show me where to go in the evening. I put my stuff away in the bureau and made up my bed. Then Bridgette said, "Come with me, let's go down to the homeroom."

My little group of homies was doing their homework when I arrived. I saw Jackie and a pretty girl named Karen and noticed Susie and Debbie were wearing tons of make-up, and tight jeans. Another girl called Eva, who was more understated, also said hello to me. They were all using signs and a little bit of voice so that I could understand them. Soon we were all talking to each other. I discovered that Debbie was hearing but knew sign language. I was confused. How did she get into Boston School? Debbie explained that she had aphasia, which meant she had trouble with auditory senses and had to rely on sign language and her visual senses. I never quite understood that. We got along immediately because we communicated the best. Debbie gave me a quick rundown of all the boys; who was cool and who to avoid.

Then we went to the cafeteria for dinner. Some boys I hadn't seen before sat at our table. Debbie introduced me to her boyfriend Todd and his friend Jeff. Both of them were hearing too and fluent in sign language. I didn't understand what they were doing here. Jeff stared at me and I felt electricity go through me because he was very tall and handsome with incredible green eyes. I was attracted to him right away. They were signing and talking with their voice on. The kids at the other tables had their voices turned off and were signing so fast I couldn't understand them. Then I saw Jackie and Karen running back and forth inside the kitchen to their table laughing. I didn't get the joke or what was so funny. Something was going on and I sensed it involved me. I asked Debbie why all the girls were acting that way. She shrugged her shoulders, saying, "I have no idea."

Todd said, "Why don't you guys come to our room and watch TV with us tonight?"

"Sure," I replied, trying to play it cool.

We hurried back to our dormitory to get dolled up for our visit. I went to Debbie's room and saw her putting more make-up on, so I decided to do the same. I thought she was putting way too much blush on her cheeks. Then she added some dark-purple eyeshadow and dark-red lipstick. She looked like a hooker, but I didn't tell her that. Next she unbuttoned her shirt down to her bra. I thought it was way too much. I'd be embarrassed to be seen in public with her. Finally she sprayed herself down with perfume and asked me if I wanted to borrow it.

I said, "Debbie, I really wish you were my roommate."

She said, "Me too, that's a great idea. I can't stand my roommate. She has some brain damage and aphasia, and is hard to talk to. Maybe we can swap to the same room next year?"

We went to the boys' living room and immediately became the center of attention. Todd exclaimed, "Wow!" when he saw Debbie. Then he beckoned us over, saying, "Come and sit with us. We're about to watch a movie."

The lights were dimmed but I could still see Debbie and Todd make a move every time Big Ed the burly dorm supervisor left the room to check the bedrooms or go to the bathroom. Jeff was sitting right next to me and I felt so turned on by the smell of his cologne. I wanted a boyfriend so badly because I'd never had one at Duxbury High or in middle school. I felt I was owed lots of boyfriends!

Jeff asked questions to find out more about my life. I answered him as best I could and blushed every time he looked at me. My heart was racing when he touched my thigh and stroked it. I could feel the warmth of his hand through my jeans. I wanted to kiss him but thought I'd better not, as we had just met.

Big Ed turned on the lights and told us to go back to our dormitory because it was late. We got up and walked giddily away. Todd ran up behind us, pretending he was going to make a phone call halfway down the hall, but instead he grabbed Debbie's waist and kissed her on the lips in front of me. I thought, *Wow, how lucky she is*.

Back in the girls' dormitory I saw that most of the girls had already got their pajamas on and had showered, because there was steam coming from the bathroom. I needed a shower too but it was 10pm, which was lights out. However, the dorm supervisor made an exception as it was my first day. I hurried into one of the cubicles, washed my hair, dried myself and put my new pajamas on. I was so tired and couldn't wait to go to sleep. I slid down under my comforter and felt something slimy and wet on my legs. I reached over to my little lamp to see what it was. Then I lifted up the comforter and saw ketchup, mustard, mayo and raw eggs all over the sheets. I shrieked in horror. Why would someone do this to me? I burst into tears and screamed, "Why? Why? Why?"

Jane, the dorm supervisor, came running in and turned on the main light. She looked horrified and demanded to know who had ruined my bed. Bridgette shook her head and said she had no idea who was behind the prank. So Jane woke up all the girls and made them come into the room to look at the mess. They tried to look concerned but then burst into fits of giggles. Debbie came over and said, "Oh no! I had no idea that they would do this while we were gone."

Then Jackie and Karen stepped forward and admitted they had put the stuff on the sheets because it was a tradition to mess up the new girl's bed. Jane shouted, "You have no right to do this to Jennifer. There are very few new arrivals here and no tradition of doing such a thing." She made them get clean sheets and remake the bed for me. I took another shower, sobbing as I washed off all the sticky mess. Why couldn't I just meet people who didn't bully me like this? I felt depressed all over again, just like old times.

Jackie came into the bathroom and apologized in sign language. I replied, "Okay" but I didn't trust her anymore. At around midnight I climbed into bed and tried to sleep, wondering why they had done this so soon after meeting me. How could they turn against me so fast?

The next morning everyone was talking about what had happened. David caught me on the way to class and tried to cheer me up by making goofy faces. All day students came up to me and said, "Don't worry about it too much. It was just a stupid joke." I went over to Randolph High and I saw Jeff standing near my locker, smiling at me. I smiled back and then went to my class. Maybe there was hope after all.

Chapter 12

Finally, the event I had been waiting for arrived. It was dance night. Students from other deaf schools and those who had graduated had been invited too. I couldn't wait to see more new faces. Debbie and I walked down the long hallway and pushed our way through the swing doors to the main hall. A nun in her black-and-white robe looked at me and smiled as I walked past her. That was a good omen.

A long line of smartly dressed kids stood near the front entrance of the school waiting to get into the dance hall. Almost right away I saw David, who approached me with a red carnation in his hand and said sweetly, "This is for you." I thought, *Gosh! I have never been treated like this before.* Then I saw Jeff standing in the corner glaring at him with jealousy written all over his face. He hadn't brought me a flower.

There were red and white Valentine's decorations hanging on the walls and ceilings and a red tablecloth on a table where they were selling red carnations. As soon as we arrived Debbie went off with Todd, grinning, and signed, "See you later."

To my surprise, David decided to hang out with his friends in the corner, so suddenly I found myself standing alone. Jeff made his way over and said, "Do you want to dance?" in a voice and sign language that I was comfortable with.

"Sure," I replied, and he took my hand.

Jeff was tall and lanky and had green eyes, which matched his green-and-white polo shirt. I was happy he was paying attention to me but I wished I knew more sign language so I could say more cool stuff. I noticed everyone around us was checking us out and asked Jeff why they were staring at us. He grinned and said, "It's because you're the new girl. Don't you notice how crowded it is? They all came out to see you tonight. They're curious about the new girl." I couldn't believe they would come from miles away out of curiosity. Then Jeff warned me that this is how it is within deaf culture. They needed to know everything about everyone. That was the first time I had heard about this thing called 'deaf culture.'

He asked if I wanted a drink and as soon as he had gone a couple of boys, who were twins, approached me. They introduced themselves in sign language and hand spelled their names – Steve and Sean. Sean explained that they weren't identical, which was kind of a joke as I could see that. Then he asked if I had a boyfriend. I told them, "Not yet." They both smiled. Then a pretty girl with brown, layered shoulder-length hair marched up with an angry look on her face. She grabbed Steve's arm and pulled him away. I asked Sean, "Why did she do that?" He told me that was Steve's girlfriend and they'd been dating for a long time. Her named was Karen and she shared my dormitory. She was also close friends with Jackie.

"Jackie put the eggs and sauce in your bed because she's jealous of you and thinks you'll steal her boyfriend," Sean explained. I gasped in shock that she would punish me for something she imagined I would do. After a couple of minutes Jeff came back with my drink and signed something super-fast to Sean. Whatever he said it made him go back to his friends.

My eye was drawn to the most attractive girl in the room, wearing a beautifully coordinated outfit. She was standing with a very good-looking boy and talking to a group of people. I could tell this couple was high up in the ranks within the deaf community. Jeff told me her name was Lorie and she was with her boyfriend, a senior called Bob. They had been dating since middle school.

I was right. These two were like royalty around here. I found out she was very deaf and didn't speak at all, but used sign language very beautifully with her perfectly manicured hands. I felt envious that she had acquired such an amazing skill compared to me, with my slow clumsy movements. Plus she had this tall handsome dark-haired boyfriend, wearing a jacket with a letter on the back, which meant he was on the basketball or soccer team. She had her hand on his arm as they walked around. I couldn't believe what a gentlemen he was and how he treated her with such kindness. I didn't learn until later that she had Usher syndrome, which would eventually cause her to go blind as she aged. She was holding onto his arm because she couldn't see very well in the dim light.

David finally came over and asked if I wanted to dance with him. I accepted his invitation and left Jeff looking disappointed as we walked off. While we were dancing I imagined that he would become my boyfriend. He was tall, funny and I liked his cologne. My romantic thoughts were abruptly interrupted when the lights were suddenly turned on and the staff signed that dance night was over. Everyone inched slowly towards the door, still talking to their friends in circles. It took forever for them to finally leave. The lights were flicked on and off to get their attention. I learned that it was part of the deaf culture to talk as long as possible.

I was so excited that I'd met a couple of boys that I liked. Debbie was all flushed and happy when she found me waiting for her in the hallway. Her make-up was smudged around her eyes and there was no lipstick on her mouth because she'd been making out with Todd all evening. On our way back to the dormitory Debbie asked me over and over, "Do you like it here?"

"Yes, I love it and can't wait to have a boyfriend who really cares about me and treats me right."

"With your beautiful perfect looks you'll have boys fighting over you," she replied.

"No, I'm not pretty. Everyone at my old school said I was ugly."

Debbie was shocked. "Are you crazy? You are a gorgeous-looking girl. Why do you think boys came up to you? And David, who's one of the most popular boys in school, gave you a red carnation."

That night I felt my self-esteem was boosted slightly and hoped my friend was right. Since kindergarten I had had it drummed into my head that I was big and horrible-looking and I still believed it.

Chapter 13

When I got on the bus to Randolph High, Lorie's boyfriend Bob was standing between the seats holding onto the grips above. There was no room to sit down because I'd arrived late. I was nudged and pushed down the bus and ended up a few inches away from him. We locked eyes and smiled. All the passengers were scrutinizing us and watching our hands.

"Where are you from?" I asked him. He told me he was from Scituate, a town in Plymouth County. He drove back and forth to school every day. I was impressed that he had his own car. He also told me he worked for a lobster company part-time, making traps. My Italian Grammy Bruno made the best stuffed lobsters. It's my favorite food in the world. So we had something in common!

I held onto a hand grip and looked right into his eyes. He looked so hot, with the muscles in his arms tensed and bulging. He was tall and lean, with thick black hair, dark eyelashes and green eyes. He was definitely my type but Lorie was his long-term girlfriend, so I couldn't think about him that way.

The twins poked him in the back and told him to stop looking at me. They reminded him about Lorie and signed a warning into his face over and over. I instantly knew that she would hear about this. In deaf culture you must report everything that you have seen to everyone. Then this weird hollering noise started. It was directed at Bob. The bus driver shouted to everyone to be quiet, which was hilarious because everyone was deaf and couldn't hear him or gauge how loud they were being.

Finally we arrived at Randolph High. Jeff was standing in front of my locker with a smirk on his face. I blushed and said, "Hi, I'm surprised to see you here waiting for me."

He came right back with, "Do you want to come to my dorm on Monday?"

Then I saw David standing in the doorway. I totally forgot about Jeff every time I saw David and wished he would ask me out. He lived twenty minutes away from my house so it would be easy to see him at weekends. He smiled, grabbed my hand and then pulled it jokingly. I pushed him away and laughed because this was his idea of flirting with me. A couple of the other boys copied him, thinking it was some kind of game, and got hold of my waist and hands. I kept saying, "Stop!" but they just kept jabbing at me until the bell rang. I was enjoying being the center of attention, so I started to flirt with the boys to see how they would react. No one had ever showed this much interest in me in my whole life. At Duxbury High the hearing boys would grab my breast as I walked by and call me deaf and dumb.

At lunchtime I went to the cafeteria with Kathy and Joseph. I loved the grilled cheese sandwiches. I thought they were even better than my mom's. I wanted to eat two but got embarrassed if anyone saw me sneak a second one. Girls were supposed to be skinny and not look like they were eating too much. I got my lunch and sat with Kathy at a bench next to one of the long metal picnic tables.

As I was enjoying my grilled cheese, a deaf girl named Julie came up to me and angrily signed, "You're a whore."

At first I didn't understand what she said so I asked Kathy to spell it out for me. When I learned what she had called me, I said, "Why did you call me that?"

"You're having sex with all my friends' boyfriends behind their backs," she replied.

"That's not true!" I protested. "I never had sex with any of them and would never do that. I'm still a virgin."

Julie responded by using the letters of my name, 'J' and 'B' and then the word 'whore' to form a new sign near her cheek. I felt a stabbing pain in my heart. Then she turned around and went to join a group of girls. She said something to them and they started jeering at me and making rude gestures. I sat down in tears. Kathy kept finger spelling to me to ignore them because she knew I wasn't sleeping around.

At the end of the day, some of the deaf students came up to me, signing the disgusting new name Julie had created. Soon everyone was using my name 'Jennifer Bruno' to mean 'whore' and signing next to their cheek. David saw me in the hallway in tears. He told me to relax and calm down, and tried to reassure me. "You have no clue about deaf culture," he said. "It's their way of warning you off their boyfriends because they can see you're getting all the attention."

"But why have they already made up their minds about me? Why would they invent such a cruel sign, calling me a whore?"

I came to school wearing a beautiful outfit: white pants, a long pink silk shirt and a pretty pearl necklace and bracelets because I had a job interview up the street from the school at the local pizza place. It happened to be my birthday that day and everyone at school knew it.

I got on the blue bus to go sit in the back seat. Cathy D tapped me on the back to make me turn around. She was with Jackie who was sitting behind her. Immediately I was suspicious because Jackie was the one who had put food in my bed on my first night there.

Cathy had a dark chocolate cupcake in her hand with an unlit candle stuck in the frosting. They both started to sing to 'Happy Birthday' in sign language while everyone on the bus watched with worried looks on their faces. All of sudden Cathy pushed the cupcake forcefully into my face. I started to fall backwards and wiped chocolate all over my new silk shirt trying to keep my balance.

I was horrified and put my hands up to push her away, then started to cry in front of everyone. I started screaming at her, "Why?" over and over again. I was so distraught that I rushed off the bus. I cried all the way to the bathroom to wash my face and blouse. Then I went to the nurse to say I was sick and had thrown up on my shirt because I didn't want to go to any classes. I couldn't bring myself to report what had happened for fear that the whole school would bully me again. I was devastated. Once again, I wanted to kill myself and disappear from the face of the earth. I couldn't wait to go home for the weekend.

Later that day my dad's car pulled up. As I got in he smiled and said, "We missed you this week. I'm glad you're going to be with us for a couple of days." I tried to put a smile on my face and act normally. I had been telling my parents how happy I was all week and didn't want to disappoint them. I was stuck between the hearing and deaf worlds. When would I ever stop being bullied? Maybe I wasn't pretty enough. All the really attractive girls seemed to have great lives. If I was hearing, I would have been a cheerleader and gone to medical school to become a heart surgeon or studied to be a lawyer. I wished I wasn't deaf so I didn't have to deal with any of this.

Monday came too quickly. Dad dropped me off at school and said he'd take me out for dinner that week. As I was walking to the front steps I caught sight of some girls making the 'whore' sign against their faces repeatedly. I avoided all of them and went straight to my homeroom.

That evening in our dorm room, Debbie was getting ready to see Todd in the boys' TV room. She was putting lots of make-up on and squealing like she'd won a lottery. She was super horny and wanted Todd to have sex with her. I tried to be happy for her but it was hard because that cruel name kept echoing in my mind.

We walked down endless hallways to the boys' dormitory at the opposite side of school. The boys didn't come to the girls' section, probably because they had a recreation room with a pool table, movie screen and couches, and we didn't. They were just getting ready to put a movie on and turn the lights out when Debbie and I arrived. Jeff motioned to me to sit next to him. I was breathless with fear and excitement because I had never sat with a boy in the dark to watch a movie.

Big Ed, the dorm supervisor, sat in front of us. He couldn't see what we were doing but I'm pretty sure he knew we were horny teenagers and were sneaking kisses behind his back. I could feel Jeff's hands all over me. Then he leaned over to kiss to my cheek. It was difficult to make out without making any noise. Todd and Debbie were all over each other and giggled every time Ed looked behind and said, "You guys better not be doing anything back there."

Jeff never asked me to go out with him at weekends or even asked me to be his girlfriend. I kept waiting but nothing was official between us. Everything I had learned about relationships was from reading my mom's Danielle Steele novels. Mom's sister Elaine was mad at her for allowing me to read adult material but I think she just wanted me to improve my English. I would devour those books in four hours straight.

I was walking back to our dorm with Debbie when I noticed a boy called Harry walking behind me. He winked at me strangely. Harry didn't speak very well, so I signed to ask him where he was from. He told me he lived way out in west Massachusetts in the country. Then he pushed me a little, which seemed to be a deaf boy's way of saying they're interested in you. I pushed him back playfully. Now I was more confused than ever. There were so many boys I liked.

Chapter 14

The Spring dance was coming up again. I was looking forward to seeing the carnations, the drinks on the table and all the decorations. Hopefully by then I'd have a boyfriend. I needed someone to hang out with during the long summer vacation. The alternative was to sit at home, bored on my own, with just my television for company.

I took the train to Boston with Eva to buy something to wear for the dance. Eva was a star player in the basketball team. She kept begging me to join the team because I was so tall. I really wasn't a sporty kind of person. I liked my hair to look pretty and my nail varnish pristine. I was a posh girl from upscale Duxbury, where the women wore expensive clothes and high heels. I wanted to get married, live in a big house, look incredible and have lots of kids, just like them.

We had found the perfect outfits at Macy's. I had chosen a black mini skirt and a white silk blouse and paired them with rows of necklaces and bracelets. On the night, Debbie went even more overboard than usual, wearing a purple ruffled shirt, tight dark jeans and black leather knee-high stiletto boots. Her make-up was more dramatic than ever. She grabbed my arm and talked about Todd the entire trek to the dance hall. I was sick of hearing about Todd; how much she was in love with him and how she planned to marry him when she graduated. Now I understood why she didn't have many friends.

As we were walking down the corridor, I caught sight of some girls signing my 'whore' name. I felt tears in my eyes but couldn't ruin my make-up so I bit my lip and carried on. Todd and Jeff were waiting for us in the dance hall. It bothered me that Jeff hadn't confirmed that he wanted me to be his girlfriend. It was the same thing with David. I didn't get it. Neither of them had made the move to ask me out. I kept wondering, *Did I do something wrong? Was I too tall for them or what?*

We all stood near the stage and watched everyone as they came in. A guy I'd never seen before came in late with a few buddies. He was very striking, with long black hair, and reminded me of Craig, the boy that I really liked who'd been killed in the motorcycle accident. He was wearing jeans, and a white shirt unbuttoned almost to the middle of his chest. I felt myself getting hot and flustered. Almost right away he saw me and we locked eyes.

I knew everyone was watching us like hawks. Despite the public gaze he came over and talked to me in voice and sign language. He could talk like me! He introduced himself as Jim D. I said my name was Jennifer and signed the letter 'J' in mid-air. I could smell his cologne, as it was very strong. Oh my, I was so attracted to him. Without any hesitation he said, "Wanna dance?" I loved how self-assured he was. The music had just started and people were already moving onto the floor. He was easily the hottest guy in the room and I was so impressed that he had made a move on me already.

As the evening drew to a close the tempo changed. Jim D put his arms around me, fixed me with his eyes and kissed me passionately on my mouth. I was floored. He was the first boy to ever make such a ballsy move. The girls all stood around pointing at me and signing that nasty name. Jim D kissed me for the rest of the night and I totally forgot about them and Jeff.

When the lights came on he grabbed a piece of paper and quickly wrote down his TTY number. I tore a piece off the bottom and gave him mine. A TTY is a text telephone designed for the deaf. It lets people who can't hear or speak clearly type messages to one another. The school TTY was set on a small wooden table desk located inside a tight phone booth for privacy. My parents also had one in the kitchen.

Jim told me to call him every night. He didn't want to let go of me and wanted to stay and chat, but the staff were telling everyone to move it. We clung on to every last minute we had together before we had to leave. It was love at first sight for me and for him too. There was no doubt in my mind that we would get married.

As soon as I got home on Friday, I went to the TTY machine on the kitchen countertop, near the regular corded phone. Jim D was so excited to hear from me and we made plans to see each other at the weekend. My parents had never seen me this cheerful, so they didn't interfere. I told them I was going out on Saturday night with my new boyfriend and a couple of his buddies. I didn't tell them we were going to his friend's house in Boston and then to a rooftop bar above a funeral home.

I put on my favorite black mini skirt and a white top. I always wore black or white and my dad would tease me about my closet having nothing colorful in it. Jim D came to the front door and I introduced him to my parents. He handled everything nicely by talking to my parents in voice. Mom tried to sign as well as speak as she wanted to make him feel welcome.

His buddies sat in the back seat of the car and I sat up front. They dressed differently to him, in jeans and black leather vests. They looked like they belonged to a motorcycle gang. I finger spelled my name to them because they were both severely deaf. I was told there had been a change of plan and they were going to a party at his friend's house, whose parents had gone away for the weekend. Jim D warned me there would be alcohol and weed there. I wanted to appear cool, so I replied, "Yeh, whatever, I'm fine with that." I was a little nervous about going over there. It was about an hour away to Rhode Island via the back roads.

Jim D introduced me to his crowd and to a girl named Suzanne who could talk and sign at the same time like me. I followed her into her parents' kitchen and she poured alcohol into some glasses. I'd never taken a drink before but I pretended it was nothing new to me and casually took a sip. I was looking for Jim D and found him laughing and fooling around, throwing pillows with his buddies in the basement. The pungent smell of weed hit me in an instant. There was no way I was joining in with that. Then he took me into a bedroom and locked the door. I wasn't ready to have sex with him because I needed to know him better and I was scared, because I was still a virgin. I didn't know what to do. We ended up making out on the bed and I could feel his penis growing hard against me. I got very tense and told him to get off.

"What's wrong?" he asked. "Can we have sex?"

I told him, "No, not yet. It's too soon."

We emerged from the room together and everyone was hollering that we'd had sex. I kept telling them, "No! We didn't do anything!" but they were laughing and didn't believe me. Jim D went outside to smoke some more weed while I hung out with Suzanne.

She asked, "So did you do it in the bedroom?"

I replied, "Of course not. I wasn't ready and I'm not a whore like you think I am."

She said, "Relax. I'm not judging you here."

Next we headed over to his friend's place above the funeral home. I was curious to see this mysterious bar and its rooftop location. We went inside an imposing 1930s red-brick building in the heart of the city. As I walked past the dead bodies waiting to be buried or cremated the next day I burst out laughing. I thought it was so funny that we were going to a funeral home to get a drink.

We went down a dark, ornately decorated hallway, which had doors with signs for the men's and women's bathrooms. Then we climbed a curved stairway upstairs to the attic and to the bar. It was decorated with Christmas lights and had tables and chairs, a pinball machine and bottles of alcohol on a shelf. Just like the real thing, you had to pay for your drinks. I had just turned sixteen, so this was all forbidden territory for me.

I counted more than thirty deaf teenage boys signing away at each other. It was like a different world, with no hearing people. I felt so comfortable and wanted to be like everyone else who was drinking and smoking. So I decided to smoke along with them at a bar table. I didn't know how to order a drink so I asked the bartender for ideas. He said, "Try a Cape Cod. It's made with cranberry, vodka and a squeeze of lime. You'd never even know there was alcohol in it." I had a sip and before I knew it I was gulping it down because it tasted so good. I just wanted more. The guy whose parents owned the place was also the bartender and he told me I didn't have to pay for anything. Within half an hour my head was a little woozy. This was my first experience of being drunk. I badly needed to use the bathroom.

Jim D was playing darts with his friends and wasn't paying much attention to me, so I went down the winding staircase by myself and took a long pee. After I had finished I heard the bathroom door slam shut. I was the only girl there, so a wave of fear shot through me. Who had followed me in here? I opened up my stall door and was shocked to see two guys dressed in black leather biker jackets, jeans and white T-shirts, with their hair greased back. They both said hi as I walked past them to the sink. Suddenly they both grabbed me and started to kiss me. I was hopelessly drunk and went along with it. I was sandwiched between them, with one of them behind me and one in front. I was still feeling resentful towards Jim D and enjoyed my little bit of revenge, making out with two boys one at a time.

But then they pulled me down onto the floor and tried to lift up my mini skirt and pull my underwear down. With all the strength I could summon I pushed both of them off and shouted, "No! I can't do this!" I stumbled to my feet, straightened up my clothes and said, "I can't do this! I have a boyfriend, Jim D upstairs. This isn't right!"

To my surprise, both of them respected my words and backed off, mumbling and signing, "Okay … oh man."

As I was exiting the door, the more handsome of the two grabbed me and asked, "Can you consider me when Jim D dumps you?"

"What? Jim D isn't going to break up with me!" I replied.

He smirked and said, "Okay, well, he's doing something behind your back. Don't tell him I told you."

All through the school summer vacation I went out with Jim D almost every weekend, but I still refused to have sex with him. He was very patient but was becoming increasingly frustrated every time I pushed him away. One day I went over his house to hang out in his bedroom to cuddle and watch TV. We had been invited to a party and he had booked us a room in a motel because it was too far to travel back. Some of his friends were also staying there, so I agreed to go.

I called my parents and told them I was staying at a friend's house for the weekend. They didn't want me to go because it was Grammy Bruno's birthday and she'd be disappointed if I didn't show up for her birthday cookout. I felt rotten because I hadn't been to my grandparents' house for our family dinners for weeks.

Jim D wanted to take a shower before we left. While he was gone I started poking around his room because I was bored. I noticed a few letters underneath a book on his bedside table stand. I picked one of them up and my blood ran cold. It was from some girl, telling him how much she loved him and how she dreamed of being married to him one day. I looked at the dates and they had all been written while I'd been Jim D's girlfriend. There were so many letters, all written in perfect English, which meant she was probably hearing and not deaf. Jim D came out of the shower and froze when he saw me standing there with a bunch of letters in my hand.

"What is this? Are you seeing someone behind my back?"

"Well, yes I am seeing someone else," he replied nervously. "To be honest I'm confused. I don't know which one of you to choose." He told me she taught preschool kids and was hearing. She was in love with him and maybe he liked her more than me because she let him have sex whenever he wanted. I felt like I'd been slapped in the face.

"But what about all the times we talked about getting married and having a future together after I finish high school?" I protested tearfully. He got up and went to his bureau drawer and pulled out a picture of her and showed it to me. I nearly fainted! She was overweight and not pretty at all. I didn't get it.

"Wow! She isn't even attractive," I said. "What does she have that I don't?" Obviously it was the one thing I wouldn't give him. A challenge got stirred up in my mind. "Fine then," I said angrily. "We'll have sex in the motel tonight, but only if you dump her."

"Sure!" Jim D agreed immediately.

We arrived at the Quincy Motel Inn in Boston and checked in. I was so nervous because I had no idea what sex was about. His friends had already arrived and were partying in the room next to ours. The shouting and banging was so loud I had to turn my hearing aids off. Within moments, Jim D was naked in front of me. I got undressed, climbed onto the bed and waited for him to make his move. He got on top of me and I felt something hard poking at me. It was a little painful as he entered me but I was so glad it was over with. I didn't feel any excitement or pleasure because I was too annoyed about his cheating.

I quickly realized I'd made a huge mistake. Then I saw some blood on the sheets; the evidence of my lost virginity. I covered it up with a blanket while he was in the bathroom. I realized I had fallen out of love with Jim D and felt nothing for him anymore.

The next morning I put my suitcase in the trunk of his car and we headed to Wendy's for lunch. I felt a burst of fury when I saw him laughing and eating with his friends. He had got what he wanted from me and now he was ignoring me.

"Take me home!" I demanded, suddenly not feeling hungry at all.

He stared at me in disbelief and said, "I can't. I'll take you back tomorrow as we arranged."

"I want to go home now," I insisted. We argued back and forth and I told him that he had just used me for sex and now he wasn't interested in me. He cared more about his friends. "Your stupid buddies always have to be with you everywhere you go.

There has never been a time when we have been alone without them around," I screamed.

"Shut up!" one of them shouted.

"No, I won't shut up! You're all as bad as each other!"

There was no way I was going back with Jim D so he could take advantage of me again at his house. This relationship was over for good.

"You can have that teacher because you think she is better than me. Good luck with her. She works and can give you what you want. I'm not going to compete with that anymore. I'm not a whore for you to take advantage of. I'll never trust you again. This is over!" I screamed in the parking lot.

I told him to get my beaten-up pink suitcase out of his trunk so I could call my dad to pick me up. My little red pocketbook was in there that contained all my family's phone numbers. Jim D tried to calm me down and held my arm, saying, "Come on, don't be like this. I'll take you home tomorrow."

"I don't ever want to see you again! I'm better than that dumb teacher. Go away and never speak to me again!"

"Are you sure? I don't like leaving you here," he said, aware of the fact that Wendy's was in the middle of a slum neighborhood. He got in his car with one of his buddies in the passenger seat and drove away. I broke down into floods of tears next to the payphone booth. At that time there were no cellphones or pagers, people relied on ten-cent public payphones located at every gas station and fast food restaurant. Luckily I had a few coins and realized my parents were not that far away. I looked for Grammy's phone number and prayed that someone would answer.

"Hello?" I could just make out my Grammy's voice as it was hard to hear anything through the receiver. I told her I wanted to speak to my dad.

She said, "Wait a minute, I'll go and get him." I heard that part but missed most of what she was saying. Then I composed myself and took some deep breaths as I didn't want to sound like I was crying.

"Hey dad, I need your help. Can you give me a ride back home or take me to Grammy's?"

I gave him the street name and he started talking but I couldn't make out any of it, just the words, "Stay where you are and I'll be there in a few minutes."

I waited for what seemed like forever until a shiny white Cadillac pulled up. Uncle Jimmy was driving his new car with Dad up front and my cousin Kristin sitting in the back. Dad hugged me and asked if I was alright. "I'm fine," I replied as casually as I could. "There was a change of plans and I decided not to stay at my friend's house this weekend. Please don't ask me why."

As we were driving, Dad turned around and said, "Please take off those earrings and get that make-up off your face. You look a mess." I tried my best to remove my smudged make-up with a tissue I had in my purse. I sprayed a little perfume on my clothes and took my long dangly earrings off.

With all my relatives, and a cookout going on the grill, I soon forgot what had happened with Jim D. Grammy came up to me and grabbed me by the cheeks and gave me a big hug. "I'm so glad you're here to celebrate my birthday. You know that I am more important than your friends. Shame on you!" she scolded, shaking her finger at me.

I laughed and said, "Of course you are more important. That's why I changed my mind and came here." It was wonderful to hang out with my cousins and enjoy all the delicious food. There were stuffed lobsters, grilled steaks, hamburgers, lasagna and prosciutto ham wrapped around long skinny bread sticks. It was enough food to keep you full for days.

I was heartbroken that my first boyfriend had cheated on me. To take my mind off it I watched a lot of TV in my bedroom. My mother noticed that I was back to being sad and lonely and cheered me up by taking me clothes shopping at the mall. I couldn't stop thinking about how much I wanted someone to care about me. Maybe Jeff would invite me to his home in Rhode Island. Now I knew how to drive I could go visit him.

Chapter 15

It was a new school year and this time I was going back as a junior. Debbie was my roommate and she jumped up and down when she saw me arriving. We got the last room at the end of the hallway. I'd told her to get there early to grab that one because it the furthest away from the dorm supervisor's room, which meant we could sneak outside for a smoke or fool around without being told to be quiet.

I made up my bed with my new comforter set and put all my clothes, make-up and books away. I asked Debbie if she had seen Todd during the summer. She said she hadn't and I was really taken aback.

"How can you trust him? What if he gets another girlfriend behind your back?"

She replied breezily, "Oh, I trust him. We talk over the phone every day."

Debbie asked me what happened with Jim D and I filled her in with all the details. I was still full of rage, thinking how he took advantage of me. I'd lost my virginity to that cheating jerk. Her eyes widened as I relayed my story. Then she smiled and reminded me, "There's always Jeff." I told her Jeff was lame and never wanted to see me at weekends. He was probably seeing someone else anyhow and didn't want me to know about his secret life.

"Anyway, I don't care anymore. I'm here for my education, not boys."

"Yeh, right, of course you're not," Debbie laughed. "I bet you'll have a new boyfriend within a week."

As I was sitting down, I saw Sean grinning at me. He came over and said, "Hey, I have a question for you. Did you break up with Jim D?"

I replied, "Yes, we are officially broken up. I'm single again."

"Oh great!" he smiled, "I'll see you around." A typical deaf culture move, I thought, prying into everyone's business. I saw Sean signing to his buddies at the table. They all turned and waved at me.

Debbie couldn't wait to tell me about the new situation over in the boys' dorm. Todd and Jeff were now roommates and had earned special privileges, so now they had their own apartment with a private living room, TV and mini fridge.

"Do you know what this means? We can go see them without anyone watching what we're doing," Debbie exclaimed, her eyes sparkling with delight.

"I'm not going, sorry," I said, bursting her bubble.

"What? Are you serious?"

"Nope, I'm not going. I don't want to be with Jeff. He's never made a move towards me or even given me his phone number. I'll hang out with the boys in the senior girls' privileges room."

True to my word, I went to join their crowd. I peeked through the door and asked if I could go in. They waved and shouted

"Sure!" First to catch my eye was Harry, who was chatting with some senior girls. He was joined by Derrick, who had dark hair and a neatly trimmed mustache. Within minutes Derrick was flirting with me quite aggressively. Harry signed with his finger slashing his throat, which meant Derrick was no good. Harry wasn't as handsome as Jim D, David or Jeff but he had lots of self-confidence. He told Derrick to leave me alone. It was like watching a rocket launch as Derrick got angry. He was all set for a fight, when one of the senior girls told them she would get into trouble for having so many people in her room. Then she told Derrick to get out.

Harry looked at me and explained, "No one likes him. He has a massive temper and loses it over stupid things real fast. He picks fights with other students and the teachers." I was really thankful that he had protected me. He winked at me and said, "Do you want to go out with me this weekend?" I gave him my address, smiling to myself that Debbie had been wrong about it taking a week to find a new boyfriend. It had only been a couple of days!

"I'll walk you back to girls' dormitory," he said, taking my hand. At the foot of the stairs, when no one was looking, he leaned over and gave me a quick kiss on the lips. I ran all the way up the long dark curved staircase to my room on the fourth floor and waited for Debbie. When she returned she looked the same as she always did after seeing Todd. Her make-up was smeared and her lipstick had completely disappeared.

I said to Debbie, "Guess what? Harry kissed me!"

Debbie screeched, "I told you! I said you'd get another boyfriend quickly."

"Oh no, he's not my boyfriend yet. He hasn't asked me out or anything."

"He doesn't have to ask you because he has already kissed you, which means you are officially his," she stated.

"No way, I don't think so."

"By the way, Jeff asked for you and was very surprised you didn't show up. You should have seen his face. He looked so disappointed when I told him you had refused to visit with me." Debbie went to shower and left me wondering how I was going to handle all this attention. All my problems would be solved if only one of these guys would step up and tell everyone we were dating.

The next day Harry had saved me a seat next to him on the bus. As the students walked past a few of them congratulated me, saying, "Great news! I hear you're a couple now," and "Nice!" and giving me the thumbs-up. I looked at him, confused as to why they were making such comments.

He smiled and said, "I have told everyone we're officially together. Nobody can take you away from me."

I saw Harry all the time and we started to hold hands together in the hallways. Sometimes we'd go to Sue's room and cuddle on the couch, watching a movie or a show. This went on for about two months. One day Harry asked if I'd like to go to a party at a motel with him. He drove me to a tiny motel in Braintree at the side of the highway. I was all dressed up and so excited to see our deaf friends who were coming from Rhode Island as well as the Clarke and Boston deaf schools. Some older students who had graduated had rented three consecutive rooms with balconies so we could go back and forth between them. As some of them were older than twenty-one they showed up with twelve-packs of beer and put them in the bathtub with some ice.

Harry took me to the liquor store to buy some cinnamon schnapps because I didn't like beer. At the time there were no strict laws about showing ID and I looked older than twenty-one, even though and I was only eighteen. I picked out a six-pack of wine coolers and pointed at a bottle of hard liquor behind the register and said, "I'll have that too." The man at the counter didn't question me as I paid and I tried not to giggle as I left the store.

Harry dumped all of the beers into the bathtub with the others. I had never seen so much alcohol in my life. He then proceeded to knock back one bottle after another. I counted seven in two hours. I thought, whoa, that's way too many for one person. Then he started acting very weirdly and kissing me all over my face. All of sudden he ran to the bathroom and threw up in the toilet, leaving vomit all over the seat and floor. I felt sick to my stomach with the stench and thought I had to leave before I threw up myself.

At that second I fell out of love with Harry. I couldn't handle someone who drank like a lunatic. He had told me how much he loved beer and drank every weekend and had even bragged about how much he vomited. I thought he was joking. I didn't want a boyfriend with smelly leftover puke in his mouth. His behavior reminded me of my mom's alcoholic dad. I didn't want to be like my grandmother and pretend that was normal.

Harry came over to me in the corner and tried to kiss me. I refused because he'd just thrown up. How gross is that? I pushed him away and told him, "I don't want to be with you anymore. You're not my type."

He burst into tears, pleading, "Oh my god, please no! I really love you and want to be with you." I wanted to go home but Harry was far too drunk to drive. I couldn't call my parents because they'd be furious I was at a motel. So I went to another room and was relieved to see Bob, the good-looking guy who had been dating Lorie last year.

"Hi!" he said, coming right up close to my face. "What are you doing here?" I explained that I had just broken up with Harry because I didn't like the way he vomited. Bob laughed at the way I said 'vomit.' I stared at his green eyes and felt a powerful chemistry between us. We started to kiss.

"Sleep with me tonight in other motel room," he said. I knew he was sharing with a group of friends so I wasn't worried that he was trying to get me into bed. Suddenly I felt a tap on my shoulder. Lorie was signing at me furiously and making angry noises. I had no idea what she was saying. She gave Bob a look of disgust and then dug her nails deeply into his arm drawing blood. I wrenched her off him, pulled her hair and hit her. All the boys, including the twins, shouted at me to leave her alone. She had Usher syndrome and her eyesight was bad, so it wasn't really a fair fight. They pushed Bob and me out of the room and I ended up sleeping with him on the floor, along with a bunch of other people.

Bob motioned to me to go to the bathroom with him. He locked the door, took his clothes off and asked me to do the same. We started making out like crazy, while touching each other at the same time. Then I got on top of him and we had sex in the tub. It felt so good because he was the hottest and most popular guy in the school. I really thought Bob would be my next boyfriend.

I woke up early and it was still dark. In the glow from the motel's exterior lights I saw bodies all over the room. I was aching from lying on the hard floor and knew I wasn't going to get any more sleep. So I went to the next motel room to find Harry and woke him up. He stared at me, trying to focus. Then he remembered we had broken up.

"I'm not driving you home," he said coldly.

"You have to drive me home now or I'll tell my parents what you did with the alcohol and you'll be in big trouble." He reluctantly got up and drove me home. My parents were waiting for me in the kitchen, visibly upset. There was no point lying because it was obvious I hadn't changed since the day before. My white blouse was stained with make-up and spilled drinks. I told them the truth. I was at a party and Harry had been too drunk to drive home and I had broken up with him because of his behavior.

"Okay, but please next time be more responsible by letting us know where you are. We have been worried sick all night. You can't hear us on the phone so we have no way of contacting you," Mom chided.

I went to my room, showered and went to bed, and smiled as I drifted off, imagining myself arm in arm with Bob. I thought how wonderful life would be with this handsome, amazing guy. Our attraction was so deep and it felt so natural for us to be together. My dreams were about to swiftly turn into another nightmare.

Chapter 16

Dad dropped me off at school on Monday on his way to work. I put my big pink suitcase in the store room and was just heading outside to go to my homeroom when I noticed some kids looking at me hatefully. Kathy got out of her cab from Rhode Island and ran up to me.

"I heard rumors that you and Harry have broken up. But the worst part is you stole Lorie's boyfriend."

"No!" I replied, "Bob told me he was no longer with Lorie. And yes, I'm pretty sure he will be my next boyfriend."

"Well you had better watch out," she warned. "Most of Harry's buddies support him all the way and think it's terrible the way you dumped him and broke his heart. All of Lorie's friends are against you too."

"That's not fair," I said to her. "I don't want to be around someone who drinks too much beer and vomits all the time."

Then a girl came up and kicked my leg, shouting, "This is for Lorie! You stole her boyfriend and you're a slut!" She signed and spat as she spoke because she was so enraged.

I was in tears trying to explain to her. "No that is not true. Bob told me he was no longer with Lorie. I would never steal someone's boyfriend. I'm not like that."

Later that day I found out that Bob was still with Lorie. He even supported her in her vendetta against me. I couldn't believe it. Everyone had turned against me. It was the worst feeling in the world; just like that time in third grade when my friends pulled my pants down at my own slumber party. I got to my classroom and was sad to see there were no boys waiting for me in the hallway. They were already inside. Harry had told them all I was a bad person and they had to ignore me.

David squirmed in his seat as I asked, "Are you on Harry's side too?"

He looked uncomfortable and signed, "Yes, I have to be because I grew up with him. You just arrived a few months ago. Let things cool down for a while and I promise we'll fool around again. Until then, stay away from me as a show of respect to my buddy Harry." I got permission to use the bathroom and sat in a stall, letting the tears drip down my face.

That night at the girls' dormitory I was in a deep state of misery. Nobody would let me explain why Harry and I were no longer together. This was going to ruin my school year. I'd have no friends because everyone was on his side. Debbie tried to cheer me up by getting me to hang out with Todd and Jeff. Jeff was thrilled to see me and welcomed me with a huge grin. He could see that I was sad and beckoned me over to sit with him. Then he got up to shut the door for privacy, jumped over the coffee table and flopped down on the couch.

"I heard what happened to you," he said. "I'm very sorry you went through that. I wished you had gone out with me and not Harry. I was going to warn you about him but I never got the chance." He looked me in the eyes and made me feel warm, but with chills of excitement too. He started to kiss me passionately. Then he finally said the words I had been waiting for. "I want you to be my girlfriend."

Even I was hesitant about the speed at which I was moving. I was jumping from one boy to another, which I learned later was because I was codependent and needed to be with someone all the time. Having been brutally teased growing up, and with such low self-esteem, it was so easy for me to fall into the wrong relationships.

Jeff and I made out all night until the 10pm curfew, when I had to go back to the girls' dorm. I didn't want to leave. I wanted to stay with Jeff in his bed but that wasn't allowed. The supervisor would do a bed count every couple of hours. Anyone who broke the rule on bed sharing was kicked out of the dormitory and had to live at home.

The next day everyone was coldly eyeballing me again. Sean came up to me when we were waiting for the bus to take us to Randolph High and asked, "Are you going out with Jeff now?" I said yes, and he laughed. "I can't believe it! You just go from one guy to the next to the next."

"Things just happen when it's the right time and the right place," I replied, trying to make my actions seem understandable.

Sean walked over to his buddies and updated them all. Harry stood there glaring at me disapprovingly. I felt so uncomfortable and tried hard to hold back my tears as I got on the bus. Jeff was waiting for me at my locker. I was delighted that he had walked over to my side of school. He hugged and kissed me in front of everyone. I didn't even care that Harry and David were watching. Jeff was paying attention to me and was officially my boyfriend. Jeff never talked about drinking beer. He was obsessed with riding his dirt bike competitively at the weekends.

David was waiting for me at the classroom door. "You need to apologize to Harry so he will treat you better and tell all of us to be nice to you," he said.

"No way!" I responded. I wasn't going to apologize to that drunk. I should have taken note of David's warning. I was frozen out for the next two months. Finally I couldn't take it anymore. I didn't even have the support of Kathy and Joseph because they were both sick at home. There was no one I could walk with, or talk to on the bus.

One day we were told by the principal that we could have lunch outside on the picnic tables as a special treat. I was trying to find someone to sit with but ended up at a table with Harry, his new girlfriend Jackie and all of his buddies. Harry yelled at me, "Go away and have your lunch somewhere else!" Immediately I felt a stab of rejection and had flashbacks of my old school where no one wanted to sit next to me. David's words echoed in my head.

Maybe it was better to apologize to Harry just to restore the peace, even though he was the one to blame for our break up. So I swallowed my pride and said, "Hey, I am sorry I broke up with you. I'm glad you have found a new girlfriend. I am really sorry for what I did. Can you please forgive me?"

Harry looked amazed and said, "Yes, sure I'll forgive you." And just like that our feud was over.

Chapter 17

The Christmas season had arrived and it was time to buy gifts for everyone. I was looking forward to giving Jeff his present before he left for the Christmas vacation. I'd been to JC Penney and picked out a couple of his favorite polo shirts, one in green and one with navy-blue stripes, and I wrapped them in a box with my mom's help. I told Debbie about Jeff's gift and how I was eager to see his reaction when he opened it. Debbie had bought Todd his favorite Polo cologne and wrapped it in a box with a blue bow.

I walked to dinner with Debbie and found Todd and Jeff were already at the table with their food, waiting for us. We were always late because we spent so much time putting on our make-up and doing our hair to look good for them. We took our food from the counter and I sat down next to Jeff.

"Guess what?" I said excitedly, "I have a Christmas gift for you to open tonight." He grinned and didn't say anything. Then Debbie told Todd she had something for him too.

Todd replied, "And I have a gift for you too to Debbie." I hoped Jeff would say the same thing to me but he didn't. He just kept staring down at his plate and continued eating. A weird sensation came over me as I tried to make sense of his awkward silence. Maybe it was true; he really did have a girlfriend at home as I had suspected.

"Why don't you come over to my house during the Christmas break?" I asked him casually. "You can pick me up and we can go away for a few days and hang out together."

He made the same excuse he always did. "I'm sorry, I can't," he said coolly. "I'm busy with dirt bike races and will be traveling to different states with my father."

We didn't have computers back then but if we had I would have Googled 'dirt bike races' and discovered the truth. It was snowing outside and no one competes outside during the winter.

Jeff smirked and said, "Actually, I'm sorry. I can't get together with you at all."

"But we have a month-long vacation!" I protested. "You can't tell me you're busy every single day!" Todd started to giggle and Debbie nudged him in the ribs. Then Debbie and I went back to the dorm to do our homework before we went to spend our free time with the boys. We hurried through our studies, put our make-up on and took our presents with us.

Todd opened up Debbie's gift right away. He thanked her and took a tiny box out of his front pocket. She opened it and screeched with delight and then hugged him tightly. It was a beautiful Irish-gold promise ring with a heart and a crown. She put it on her finger right away and showed me her hand.

I turned to Jeff excitedly. "It's your turn to open yours!"

He shook his head and said, "I don't want to open it right now. I'll wait until Christmas is over. I'll open it when I get back."

Debbie and I looked at each other. Todd remained silent and looked nervous.

"Okay," I said, trying to lighten the atmosphere. "Where's my gift from you?"

"Sorry, I forgot to bring it. I left it at home. That's why I wanted to wait until I got back with your gift. Then we can open them together."

During the Christmas vacation I was bored out of my mind, so I decided to get a job at McDonalds near my parents' house. I did the early morning shift and they called me in whenever they needed me. I was the cook in the back kitchen, flipping hamburgers and deep-frying the French fries, chicken nuggets and fish filets. I loved making the salads and the fresh breakfast biscuits in the morning. My new job took my mind off all the problems I was having in my relationships. I seemed to be attracted to all the wrong kinds of boys. Why couldn't I find someone who would treat me properly, like the heroes in my Danielle Steele books?

Chapter 18

When I returned to school in the New Year I had totally forgotten about my Christmas present sitting on Jeff's shelf. There it was in plain view in his living room when I arrived.

"How was your Christmas vacation?" I asked. "And how did your dirt bike competitions go? It must have been so cold riding outside. Did you get hurt at all?

Jeff grinned and said, "No, I was okay."

"So why don't you open my gift? It's sitting right there."

He looked at me uncomfortably and said, "I'm sorry I forgot to bring yours. Can we wait until next week?"

"I don't care about my gift," I said tensely. "Can you please just open it now because it's actually embarrassing to see it still there. Christmas was over weeks ago. It's January now."

"No, I'll leave it for a while. I don't feel right because I didn't bring you anything yet."

I told Debbie I was giving him one last chance to prove he cared for me. It was hurtful and insulting that he didn't want to know what I had thoughtfully chosen for him. We went to their room after dinner. As usual Todd gave all his attention to Debbie, treating her nicely and kissing her. Jeff just sat there and wanted nothing to do with me. Sensing the cold atmosphere, Todd nudged Debbie and they left the room, leaving us to figure things out.

I looked at Jeff and said, "I can't play your cruel game anymore. Why won't you open my present? Can you please open it?"

Jeff smiled and said, "No. I'll do it later."

"Do it now or I am breaking up with you and our relationship is over!" Suddenly Jeff grabbed a pair of tiny nail scissors from his coffee table, held my right wrist and slashed it with the open side of the blade.

"Go ahead and die!" he sneered, with hatred in his eyes. Then he grabbed my neck and started to choke me.

I kicked him off, screaming, "How dare you! You're nasty! I never, ever want to see you again!" I ran as fast as I could to the girl's dorm. I was shaken up and crying. Why would Jeff hurt my wrist and choke me? I didn't know what to do. I was afraid to tell the supervisor because everyone in the school would support Jeff, as they grew up with him.

The following day I avoided him. On the bus going over to Randolph High, Kathy and Joseph noticed something was wrong because I looked so sad. They kept saying, "Please cheer up. Don't worry about Jeff. He's a loser."

I walked to my locker and saw Jeff there with two of his buddies. I told him, "Go away and don't ever come near me again or I'll tell everyone what you did to me!"

Jeff said, "If you do that, I'll make sure all of my buddies and everyone in school turns their back on you. You will have a miserable school year." He followed me to my class, looking threatening in his long black trench coat, black sunglasses and black hat. Then he watched as I sat at my desk and stood next to me, giving me the evil eye. Finally the bell rang and he walked off before the teacher came in. But he wasn't done with terrorizing me. He found me in the cafeteria and stared at me while I was eating my grilled cheese sandwich.

"Please go away," I begged. "You will never be my boyfriend ever. Please leave now."

"No," he replied. "I will keep bothering you every day until you give in and say you'll get back with me."

For three weeks straight he harassed me in his sinister long black trench coat. I had so much anxiety I was sure I was headed for a nervous breakdown. Nobody dared to talk to me while he was around. After another day of hell I told Debbie, "I can't do this anymore. I don't want to be here at this school. I am going to swallow a bottle of aspirins. Please don't tell anyone."

I just wanted to die in my sleep so I wouldn't have to deal with Jeff and his terror tactics, or with being frozen out by his buddies. I was obviously worthless or I wouldn't have been treated so badly by Jim D, Bob, Harry and now Jeff. I never wanted to commit suicide. I only wanted to get out of my awful situation. So I pretended to swallow a handful of pills but only swallowed two. I went to sleep and was shaken awake about an hour later by supervisor Jane. Debbie was standing next to her.

"Wake up!" she shouted, slapping my face gently.

I kept telling her, "Go away and leave me alone." All of a sudden the room was filled with firemen, police and paramedics.

I was put on a stretcher and taken to the hospital. I looked at Debbie on the way out and she had tears running down her face.

"I'm sorry, but I had to save your life by telling Jane. Please forgive me. I am so sorry." I was carried down the long, curved staircase and taken to the ambulance. Everyone was peering out of the dormitory windows, fascinated by the drama outside.

They put me in the emergency room and a nurse, who I will never forget, looked at me and asked, "Why would you do this? You are such a beautiful girl. You shouldn't want to kill yourself." Doctors, nurses and techs all crowded around me, taking my vitals and checking me out. Then they forced charcoal up my nose and into my stomach, which was extremely uncomfortable, as they thought I had taken twenty pills.

About an hour later, my parents rushed in. Dad looked at me and asked, "Why?" I couldn't respond and just stared into space, numb with sadness, while they tried to comfort me by holding my hands and stroking my hair.

I was allowed to go back home in the early morning hours. Once again I was back in my bed, looking up at the ceiling. I didn't know what to do and how I was going to face everyone at school or cope with Jeff. Then my mother opened my door and said she had been on the phone and had talked to a psychologist about my situation. "There's a hospital where you can get help. They do counseling and therapy for kids with problems," she said.

I had never heard of such a place and had no idea what this meant. "How long do I stay there?"

"It depends. Sometimes weeks or months, depending on how well you recover."

Great! I thought. Now I didn't have to deal with Jeff or anyone at school. Jeff was graduating early in May, before the juniors, sophomores and freshmen, which was three months from now.

"I'd love to go," I responded enthusiastically. "But what about my homework? I don't want to repeat a year."

"You don't have to worry about that," she assured me. "I called the school and they will give us your homework and we will bring it to the facility for you to do."

"Okay, I want to go," I confirmed and started packing my clothes and other belongings.

Chapter 19

My dad drove me up a long winding road to a quaint old building situated in the middle of woods in Pembroke. I hugged my parents and said goodbye. My mother was in tears as she left.

I was taken to meet with the nurses at Pembroke Hospital. One of them explained that now I was here I had no freedom, wasn't allowed to go outside and that all the doors were kept locked to prevent anyone escaping. What? I had no idea what I was getting myself into. I was too young to understand what a psychiatric hospital was. I didn't take all those aspirins. I was just depressed and acting out. I never wanted to kill myself. I wanted to live to a hundred years old.

Little did I know that this was just the beginning of a whole new dark and twisted chapter of terror and I was about to meet someone who would change my life in the most frightening and horrendous way. I deeply wish now that I had not agreed to go there. It is probably the biggest regret of my life.

The nurse finished off her speech by saying, "Now a tech will show you around. You're going to a maximum security room downstairs, which means you'll be locked up all day until we think you have improved. Then you'll be transferred upstairs where there's a bit more freedom."

A handsome older tech called Rob winked at me and said, "I've come to take you downstairs." He kept shooting me glances as we made our way along the corridor. "Hey, you're too beautiful. You shouldn't be here," he said.

"So why was I called ugly my whole life at school?" I replied. I'm sure he was just saying that because he felt sorry for me being deaf.

"Oh, they are jealous. They just pick on you because it makes them feel better. Surely you know that bullies are just losers?" he said.

I peered through a small square glass window in the door. I could see a huge living room full of comfortable-looking couches and chairs. There were round table and chair sets in dark purple, lime green and bright orange colors. Then the tech told me there was a small smoking room with a TV directly opposite the nurses' station.

"Practically everyone in here smokes," he said, adding, "There's a lighter attached to a cord fixed to a desk in the nurses' station. You light your cigarette in there before you go in the smoking room. They don't allow you to have matches or lighters." I thought that was so cool. He quickly showed me my room, which was basically a twin-sized bed in a small rectangular room.

"Your suitcase is being checked right now," he said. "You'll get your stuff later. The next thing that will happen is you'll be called to see a psychiatrist to discuss your case and get your medication."

What? No! I didn't need medication. There was nothing wrong with me! I'm only here because I wanted to get away from Jeff. But then I remembered. I had to stretch this out for at least three months until Jeff had graduated, so I had to pretend to be suicidal and take their pills.

A boy around my age, with bad acne and curly brown hair, wearing round wire-framed glasses, beckoned me over, saying, "Hi! Come and sit down with me." I plopped down onto a huge stuffed pillow on the floor. "My name's Mickey and what's yours?" I told him and then I asked what he was doing here. He replied, "Well, I tried to hang myself. I'm tired of this life and I want to die."

"No, you got a whole life ahead of you. Please don't do that," I said, unaware of how ironic that sounded.

"So why are you here?" I told him about my situation with Jeff and Harry and that I had got depressed and taken some pills. He stared at me and said, "You shouldn't have any problems. You are the most beautiful girl here."

A stunning girl with long blond hair walked over and sat down. She said something to Mickey, which I didn't understand. Then she looked at me directly because Mickey had told her I was deaf and she introduced herself as Sarah. We hit it off right away because she was so friendly and funny. I asked why she was here and she leaned over and said, "This is a secret but I'm getting away from my stepfather who is sexually touching me. I don't want anyone to know so I pretended to kill myself."

We became great friends and were always together. We'd go into the mini kitchen and throw plastic forks at each other or sit on the countertop and talk. The techs would check on us, peering through the window every twenty minutes. The only thing that separated us was when it was time for counseling appointments and a tech escorted one of us upstairs.

My psychologist Samantha was slim and tanned, wore nice clothes and high heels. I wanted to be like her. I told her all about my life, how I didn't understand anything in school with no interpreter, how I was called ugly every day and had been relentlessly bullied. I told her about Jeff, Bob, Jim D and Harry. Then I confided that I had a diary hidden in my bedroom, which detailed everything that had happened in my life.

At my appointment the following week, Samantha told me that my mother had read my diary and brought it in to show her. I hated Samantha and my mother for doing this to me. I yelled at her, "You have no right to do that! You had no right to tell my mother where my diary was!" I picked up some knick-knacks from her desk and started throwing them at the wall.

"This behavior is unacceptable. I'm calling the techs to restrain you!" I was still yelling at her when four strong guys rushed in, took hold of me and threw me over their shoulders. They carried me downstairs and put restraints on my ankles and wrists. I felt the nurse put a long needle in my butt and I fell asleep right away.

I woke up feeling very drowsy. Then I saw my friends looking through the tiny window in my door. They were trying to talk to me but I couldn't read their lips because the glass was too smudged. Finally a tech came in and said, "Are you going to stop yelling, throwing things around and threatening people?"

I replied, "Of course I am. I was just so angry. There was no reason for you to put restraints on me. Wouldn't you be angry if someone told your mother where your private diary was and they read it?"

The tech undid the restraints, saying, "You can go now. Your friends Sarah and Mickey have been waiting in the hallway for you this whole time." As soon as I got out of the room Sarah grabbed me and hugged me. We ran to our kitchen hideaway and I told them what had happened.

"Wow, that's a terrible thing to do. You should never trust that bitch psychologist." I was so mad I told Sarah I never wanted another appointment with the psychologist again.

"You have to, otherwise they won't keep you here," she said.

Over the next few weeks we watched TV, played board games and did jigsaw puzzles. We even completed a few 1,000-piece sets, which took four days each to do. We made a pact to stay here as long as possible so we could be together, happy and safe from the awful world outside.

We were about six weeks into our stay when a muscular blond-haired guy a few years older than us arrived. His name was Devin. He was sitting in the smoking room when we came back from fooling around in the kitchen. We giggled as we opened the door, with a cigarette in our mouths, and sat down not even realizing he was there. He sat smoking nonchalantly and fixed us with a penetrating stare. Sarah asked him why he was here and he rolled up his sleeve. We all exclaimed, "Holy shit!" There were hundreds of stitches on each arm. He said he'd tried to commit suicide by slicing himself up because he'd had enough of this shit life.

"Wow, that's so brave to cut yourself up like that. You have a lot of guts; more than anyone here," I said, impressed by his total lack of fear. Then he changed the subject and started telling us crazy stories about how his friends rode their motorcycles together and raced drag cars at the weekends. He was entertaining and moved his hands a lot when he was describing the insane things he did. His voice was also very loud and clear and he didn't care who heard him.

He soon had us all giggling on the floor and I started to develop a little crush on him because I liked the way he talked, and I found his anecdotes fascinating. He was completely at ease with himself, so confident and outgoing. Most guys I knew were afraid to speak up like him. He looked at me and said in front of everyone, "You're so beautiful. I really like you."

I felt myself blushing. Sarah poked me in the ribs and said, "You should go out with him. He can be your new boyfriend."

Devin laughed and responded, "Maybe, if we get to know each other better while we're in here."

We were both sitting down, but then we got up at the same time. Oh no! He was just five feet five inches tall, while I was five feet ten. I looked down at him and said, "Oops, I'm taller than you and I didn't realize it!"

He laughed and said, "I love tall girls. I love your long legs and your long shiny hair." I felt awkward because I wanted a boyfriend who was taller than me. I didn't want to be mocked for going out with a shorter guy or have to slouch over when we slow-danced or walked hand-in-hand.

"Sorry Devin, I can't go out with you because of our height difference. Nothing will ever happen between us," I explained, hoping my direct words would make him leave me alone. But Devin continued to follow me and Sarah from room to room.

One day I saw him sitting alone with Sarah after I had gotten back from my counseling session. I felt a pang of jealousy. They were sitting right next to each other closely on a love seat in the corner, laughing and poking at each other. Devin turned to me and said, "Hey, what's happening? We were waiting for you to get back." I sat next to him, so now he was sandwiched between us.

I started talking about how I couldn't wait to get out of this overcrowded place, saying it was time for me to leave. As I was telling him how I was done with the therapy and hated my psychologist, a tech beckoned Devin to come to the phone. As he listened to whatever was being said, his face gradually contorted with fury. He began bellowing into the receiver, calling whoever it was a bitch and every other nasty name you can think of. It took four techs guys to get him away from the phone. They dragged him into the lounge to try to calm him down. Devin had turned into the Incredible Hulk and was repeatedly punching one of the techs in the face. He broke his nose and blood spattered all over his face and the walls.

A code red light started flashing. The techs upstairs came running down to assist with restraining him. In the meantime he managed to grab a chair and throw it across the room, making a dent in the wall. Sarah looked at me and gasped, "Whoa! What a strong person he is to fight like that."

It took eight people to hold him down and put restraints on him. Then a nurse stabbed him hard with a needle in his shoulder and they took him to his room and tied him to the bed. He must have been there for two days, but I didn't care because I wasn't interested in him. I couldn't believe that he'd given one of the techs a black eye and broken another one's nose.

When he was finally let out of his room he acted like nothing had happened and followed me around from the smoking room to the living room and to kitchen again. Then he came up to me with a teddy bear and bouquet of red roses and said, "These are for you. I got my foster dad to bring them in so I could give them to you."

My heart softened and I replied, "Thank you so much."

Then he knelt down on the floor with a single rose in his hand like he was about to propose and said, "Would you be my girlfriend?" I had never received attention like this from a guy and it was so passionate and flattering coming from such a 'bad boy.' My psychologist and my parents had warned me not to date anyone from inside the ward because they could be dangerous, but I didn't listen to them.

"Yes!" I replied happily. Everyone in the room clapped their hands. For one insane moment I totally forgot about him being too short and the fact I wasn't interested in him. How could I resist such a sweet gesture? Jeff had never given me anything at all.

He kissed me quickly before the tech arrived. There was no touching or kissing in the ward. Then he looked at me said, "We both gotta get out of here so we can start our life together. I want to marry you Jennifer. I can take care of you. I have a lot of money in the bank and my own car. I can give you everything you want."

"Are you for real?" I said, looking at his earnest face begging me to be his. I was bothered by the fact he was shorter than me, but he had a very strong, stocky body and an incredibly confident personality. There was no physical chemistry like there had been with Bob, Jim D or Jeff. My plan was to break up with him after we got out of the hospital.

"Come on over and sit with me," he said, patting the cushion beside him. Then he confided, "I was bounced from foster home to foster home all my life because no one wanted me. My parents gave me up when I was nine. They put me into care when they were going through their divorce. I felt like nobody loved me." He gripped my hand and continued, "I know you can love me because you understand how I feel. I want to marry you and I want you by my side forever. My last girlfriend went to college somewhere. She wouldn't tell me where she went."

I felt his hand tightening around mine and tried to pull away, but he wasn't going to let it go until he'd finished. "She's a bitch. I'm so angry she left me. She swore to me she would stay with me forever and she broke her promise by leaving me a letter saying she didn't love me anymore. I looked everywhere for her. No one would tell me where she was. That's why I'm in this place. I got so mad I sliced up my arms. I didn't intend to kill myself. I'm not crazy or anything. I was just broken-hearted."

"Wow," I thought, as he finally relinquished his grip. Now I wasn't sure I wanted to be with him. His arms were seriously messed up and I didn't like the mean way he talked about his ex.

A few days later I was transferred upstairs to the less-secure floor of the hospital along with my friends. We were allowed to sit outside at the picnic tables and have visitors. My mother said she would come to see me. She smiled when I entered the visitors' room and handed me a pile of cards from relatives and friends. The first thing I said to her was, "Why in the world would you read my private diary with all my secrets about my personal life?"

She stared at me in a shock and replied, "Oh no! I made your psychiatrist promise not to tell you that. She was the one that told me to read it. Wow! She lied to me."

"Well, she knows everything about my life thanks to you and I hate that you did that. How could you betray me like that! I want you to go!" I screamed. Mom was in tears when she left. I felt terrible, but she shouldn't have read it! I vowed to burn that diary when I got home.

Chapter 20

As soon as I got out of the psychiatric hospital I threw all my medication away because it made me feel like a zombie. I was happy but nervous about going back to Boston School because I hadn't been there for three months. But I was starting my senior year in the fall, with a new hearing boyfriend, and Jeff was no longer there, so that was a plus. I couldn't stay in the girls' dormitory after what I'd done, so Dad gave me his old gray 1979 Chevrolet Monte Carlo so I could commute to school every day. My parents warned me that if I screwed up and didn't come home on time or do my homework they would take the car away.

As soon as I got home from the hospital the phone rang. It was Devin. My mother answered. I turned my hearing aid up to the maximum volume and heard him asking if he could pick me up on Saturday and spend the day with me. I was interested to see how he would treat me and to find out what his car looked like. My parents weren't happy with the situation and warned me very sternly that I shouldn't pursue this relationship.

"Having a boyfriend you met in a psychiatric ward is a very dangerous thing to do. Your psychologist has told us about him and he's very bad news. He has severe mental problems. You have no idea what this guy is capable of," my mom said.

"Well, it's not a good idea for anyone to be with me either because I just came from rehab too!" I shouted defiantly. The mention of the psychologist sent me into a rage. This shut them up right away. "You can't judge anyone you haven't met. You need to let me find out who he is myself."

Saturday arrived, and I got all dressed up in tight jeans, a black shirt and my favorite thick gold-plated necklace. I looked out the window and was stunned to see an ugly old orange car pull up outside the house. It certainly wasn't the brand-new black Mustang he had described. It was a beaten-up 1974 Chevy Torino. He sat on the drive and refused to come in to meet my parents, so I went outside and sat on the dirty, trashed passenger seat. I lurched forward as he put his foot down hard on the accelerator before I had put my seatbelt on. My dad came running out of the house after me, waving his arms and shouting something, with a look of horror on his face.

Devin turned his head towards me and shouted, "Yes! We're free and we're together! We have to celebrate!"

"Yes, but I'm confused. I thought you had a black Mustang?" There was no reply.

When we got on the highway he was going well over the speed limit. I looked at the dial and saw the needle passing the 80mph mark. He was in the left lane acting like this was just a normal speed. I kept begging him, "Please slow down!"

He turned his head toward me with a weird grin and said, "Don't worry. I'm the best driver in the world. I know what I am doing. I just want to show you where I live; it's close to Boston."

"Sure," I said, trying to sound cool, but inside I was panicking and thinking, *Where the hell are we going?*

We finally arrived at a small 1950s ranch house. I got out of his car and he yelled at the top of his voice, "Wow! You're so hot! You're so beautiful!" The house interior was very simple, with basic furniture and old appliances. There was a faint smell of mold, unflushed toilets and unemptied trash bags. No one was home, so we went into the kitchen and sat at a stained wooden table.

"Let's go to my room and make love," Devin said, in his clear, deep voice. He stared at me full in the eyes in a manic kind of way, watching my every reaction. Then he pulled me by my arms towards his bed. I was really uncomfortable because I was not attracted to him at all.

"No! Seriously, no! I don't want to have sex with you on our first date and our first day out of hospital!" I said in a forceful tone.

He looked at me angrily and said, "Oh come on. Don't be an old-fashioned lady. All the girls have sex with me the first time I take them out."

I was disgusted. He was feeling me up everywhere. His fingers were prodding into my panties and into my bra. It was far too soon to have sex with him. I had no connection with him. The only emotion I had was pity for his awful life. I was nervous about who would be arriving here to find us both alone in the house together. Devin told me his foster parents had gone over to their sister-in-law's house and would be back later.

Not knowing much about him, I brought up the question about the black Mustang car. "What happened to it?" I asked again.

He looked down and said, "I lied to you. I didn't want you to think I was poor. I was trying to impress you. What am I supposed to say? I have a crappy beat-up car?"

"Well, I don't appreciate that you lied to me. That makes me feel very uncomfortable with you," I replied, shocked by his audacity.

"Can you please forgive me Jennifer?" he implored, in a fake, whiny voice. I shrugged my shoulders. A horrible feeling churned in my gut. I had never been with such an overt liar. How could I trust him? Then he changed the subject and said, "Let's go out. I need to get some ice hockey equipment. You're coming with me to Sports Authority."

He drove us there at breakneck speed, showing off and leaving black skid marks everywhere. We got inside the store and he told the clerk to help him find what he wanted. Devin pointed at the stuff hanging on the wall, saying, "I want that!" multiple times to the clerk, who would climb up a ladder and get the items down. I was amazed as he picked out ice hockey sticks, pucks, ice skates, netting, helmets … How the hell could he afford all of this stuff?

There was a huge pile on the counter. It must have been worth thousands of dollars judging by the price tags. The clerk looked delighted because he was on commission. Devin smiled and said, "I told you I had a lot of money in the bank. I can afford all this." I watched him write a check. The clerk didn't even ask him for his license to check his identity. He just accepted the payment and put it in his cash register, with a huge smile. Then he carried all the stuff to Devin's beat-up car and put it in the trunk. Devin was beaming with satisfaction and quickly drove away from the store. I discovered later that he had used a fake check. He didn't have any money in the bank according to the warrant for his arrest for fraud.

He pulled over to a park with beautiful green hills and trees and said, "Let's go for a walk near the pond." Then he pushed me to the ground and got on top of me. We rolled over each other down the hill together. He was laughing and looking into my eyes. Then he said, "I'm in love with you."

I couldn't say it back to him because it would have been a lie. I was very confused. I just wanted to go back to school and date other boys. I smiled and pretended to be happy when I wasn't, and debated with myself whether I should tell him now that I didn't want to be with him. But I didn't want to hurt his feelings as he had told me so many stories about his heart being broken. I also worried that he'd slice up his arms again if I told him I wanted nothing to do with him. So I decided to postpone that speech for now.

Chapter 21

The day had arrived for me to go back to Boston School. I drove there on my own in the hand-me-down car my dad had given me. I knew everyone would be talking about my fake suicide attempt. Literally everyone stared at me as I walked past them. Some of them said, "Hi." I kept my eyes fixed straight ahead.

My homeroom teacher Mrs. Jackson asked how I was feeling and told me she had a letter to give me. Back at the homeroom I quickly opened the envelope. It was from Jeff. He said he'd made a huge mistake treating me so badly. Then he admitted he'd been seeing a girl called Carly while I was in the hospital. He had also been dating someone in Rhode Island for years. But now he was certain I was the only one for him. He ended by apologizing again and said he wanted to marry me as soon I graduated from Boston School.

I looked at his handwritten words for a few seconds, then ripped his letter up and threw it in the trash can. I didn't want anything to do with him. I could do better. I was going to find a tall, smart, handsome boyfriend as soon as I had broken up with Devin.

David and his buddies walked past me in the corridor. He gave me a hug and we went right back to where we started, touching and grabbing each other for a laugh. He didn't say a word about my suicide attempt. Then I saw Kathy and Joe and couldn't wait to sit with them on the bus. I felt so much more comfortable when I was around them. I told Kathy I had a new boyfriend and that he was hearing.

She looked at me in surprise and asked, "Are you sure you want to be with him and not a deaf guy?"

"Yes, I feel good when a hearing guy asks me out." I didn't tell her that I was going to dump him soon.

It was a little sad and bittersweet not to be involved in dorm life. I'll never forget that old building with its antique wood-paneled hallways, long curved staircase, the heavy glass swing doors every few yards, and the massive tiled bathroom lined with shower stalls and its old-fashioned sinks and long mirrors. It was like something out of Hogwarts.

I drove to see Devin after school because he only lived about twenty minutes away. I rang the bell and he opened the door quickly to get me inside the house.

"How was school?" he asked.

"It went great. I loved it."

"Did any boys bother you at all?" he asked immediately.

"No. They're my friends, kind of like brothers to me," I reassured him.

He gave me a dark stare and then said, "Jennifer, Jennifer, Jennifer ... Make sure you don't go near a boy while you go out with me, because if you do I will kill him in plain view."

"They're my friends! There's nothing going on. We just like to tease each other and fool around," I protested.

"Jennifer!" he screeched, "You listen to me. You don't talk to any of them. I don't care if they're your friends. I'll spy on you and shoot any boys that talk to you."

I was petrified and started to shake. My father would never threaten anyone like that. What if he killed David, who'd been my pal since the first day of school? I didn't want to be around this maniac a second longer. I had to break up with him. But how was I going to tell him? He was so unstable he might flip out. I tried to think how I was going to explain to him in a nice way that I wasn't interested in him anymore. My heart was racing and my mouth was dry. I couldn't say anything. I looked around his bedroom and I saw a dark-brown faux leather photo album with gold trim. It was full of Polaroid pictures.

"That was me when I was nine years old on the ice hockey rink in my kit. I was the baddest of all. Everyone was so afraid of me. I'd fight them with my hockey stick. One time I knocked a guy out by shooting the puck in his face." He laughed so hard when he remembered the event. "You should have seen it," he cackled. "His front teeth were knocked out of his mouth and there was blood all over the ice."

He thought it was funniest thing in the world. I never heard anyone talk like that in my entire life. I wasn't used to this odd behavior. Then he turned the pages and a picture of a girl fell out of the back of the album. "That bitch! She's the one who left me. I was going to hunt her down but I don't know where she lives. I won't make that mistake again," he said ominously.

"Can I meet your friends?" I asked, trying to change the subject. He started to kiss me, but I wasn't ready to have sex with him. I pushed him away and said, "Let's go before it gets too dark. I have to go home to do my homework."

"Alright," he said. "Let's go in my car."

He drove like a maniac to a neighborhood where the roads were lined with three- story buildings. Then he pulled over into a side street where a group of guys and their girlfriends were hanging out next to some motorcycles, chatting and smoking cigarettes. Devin reached over and grabbed me by the hand as I was getting out the car and pulled me towards them.

"Hey everyone, this is my new girlfriend Jennifer. Please be nice to her and talk slow because she's deaf." Everyone smiled at me and started to talk to me but I couldn't make out what they were saying. "This is Ronnie, Nick and Billy. They're my foster brothers. I grew up with them. We're close like blood brothers. I can tell you the stories where we got into trouble, all four of us together," Devin said. They all started to laugh.

Billy's face was scarred on the left side and there were purple patches of tightly pulled skin on his neck and arms. He had been burned from a homemade bomb when he was younger. Then Nick started to howl like an animal, before jumping on his motorcycle and doing high-speed stunts, making skid marks and sending smoke all over place. The smell of burning rubber filled the air. He had absolutely no sense of danger.

Devin turned to me and said, "Nick's crazy. Completely nuts! Everyone calls him Crazy Nick."

His older brother Ronnie stood next to his pregnant girlfriend Lucy. She was a petite, dark Italian-looking girl. She had a loud mouth and kept complaining about everything. Ronnie told her to shut up and be quiet. Then he shouted, "Go get an abortion. I don't need another baby in the house!"

Billy seemed quiet and reserved. His girlfriend Dottie stood next to him and watched the others racing, swerving in circles and going up on their back wheels. Devin asked Ronnie if he could ride his motorcycle so he could show off to me.

"Sure. Don't wreck it or I'll kill you," he replied.

"Watch me!" Devin yelled in a weird, sinister voice, like a character from a horror movie. He grinned at Crazy Nick, threw his hands in the air, and screamed, "Freddie!" Then he wiggled his fingers and pretended they were attached with knives. He accelerated fast, the front of his bike reared up and he took off doing a wheelie halfway down the road. Devin and Crazy Nick raced each other up and down the street, braking hard, swerving and almost running into each other while everyone watched, casually smoking and laughing like it was no big deal.

"Are you sure you want to be with that nut?" Lucy asked me. I shrugged my shoulders and tried to laugh. But inside I was telling myself *No!*

Finally, Devin and Crazy Nick pulled over and got off their bikes. They launched themselves at each other and started mock fighting. Devin was still mimicking the character in the movie, flicking his hands up in the air and shouted menacingly, "I'm Freddie … I'm coming to get you!" It was kind of bizarre to see him behaving this way. I was slightly embarrassed because I'd never seen anyone in my neighborhood being so ridiculous. This was ghetto life and I didn't like it. It wasn't me at all. I wanted to go home to my safe pink bedroom at my parents' house in Duxbury. I kept nudging Devin, telling him I needed to go home because I had school the next day.

"Fuck school!" Devin sneered. "Fuck school. Drop out and be with me."

"No! I have to graduate! I want to go to college."

Two hours later I was desperate to leave. I had to be home before my curfew and I had homework to do. Then Devin said out of the blue, "Hey I need to know where your grandparents and everyone else you know lives. I want to meet them. Can we do that over the weekend?"

I was still waiting for the right time to tell him we were finished. "Yes, sure," I said, because I didn't want to upset him.

Chapter 22

I went to school exhausted the next day. I didn't drop get back to my house until after ten o'clock. My parents weren't happy that I had arrived home so late on a school night. I promised them from now on I'd make plans at weekends only.

I saw David with his buddies smiling at me as I was going to class. He prodded me as I walked past, to get my attention. I pushed him back and laughed.

"Are you dating a hearing guy?" he asked, with a concerned look on his face.

"Yes, it's true."

"What does he look like?"

"I'm not telling you. You'll have to find out yourself."

"Is he good to you?"

"Oh yes. He's wonderful and does everything for me," I lied.

Suddenly I remembered that Devin said he was going to spy on me in school. I stepped away from David and went to sit with Kathy and Joseph. The teacher kept glancing at me and said, "You look different, tired. There are bags under your eyes. Is everything okay?"

"Yes, everything's great," I fibbed. "I have a new boyfriend and I'm excited about it."

She looked at me and said, "Be careful. You should be focusing on your school work. You are too young to think about serious relationships."

"Yes, I know. Everything is fine," I assured her.

On Sunday my parents told me we were going to my grandparents' house for a cookout. I had asked if Devin could meet us there. I still hadn't mustered the courage to break up with him. One family gathering couldn't hurt. So I called him and gave him their address.

The grill was smoking away when we arrived and there were picnic tables and chairs lined up in the backyard. Grammy Bruno kissed me on my cheek and grabbed my chin in her rough Italian way and said, "Hey have you been a good girl?"

"Of course," I laughed. "My boyfriend will be here soon. I'll introduce you to him."

"He'd better be nice to you," Gram warned. "We'll see if he's any good." Just as she said that, I saw him limping down the driveway. He'd been in a serious motorcycle accident a few years ago, crashing into the back of a car and ended up with two broken legs. He had a steel rod in one leg, which was slightly shorter than the other.

My whole family looked at him in a shock. Nobody smiled because they had all heard about him from my parents. I was mortified. It was like I had brought a rabid dog to the house and expected everyone to pet him. I was so ashamed to introduce him to everyone. I wasn't even in love with him and didn't feel an ounce of attraction towards him.

Grammy and Grandpa Bruno went up to him and politely shook his hand. "How are you?" Grandpa asked.

"I'm fine sir," he replied. Mom and Dad were sitting on their lawn chairs with my Uncle Jimmy, looking disapprovingly at us. I ignored them and showed Devin around the house.

"Wow, everything looks so Italian," he exclaimed, noticing the carved wooden furniture with lions-claw feet, all the bronze and marble statues and dish sets from Italy displayed in the antique glass cabinets. We went back outside and sat on a couple of lawn chairs until the food was ready. As usual Grammy had produced an enormous spread, with stuffed lobsters, shish kebabs, chicken, steaks, ribs, hotdogs, hamburgers and lots of pasta salad dishes.

"I wished I had a family like this," Devin said enviously. "You're one lucky girl."

"Yes, they are my world and I love them very much," I said, smiling. "I need to go to the bathroom. I'll be right back. Are you okay sitting here by yourself?" I asked.

"Yes sure," he replied a little angrily.

No one wanted to talk to him. In fact they were all avoiding him. I went upstairs from the basement to the kitchen and saw Grandpa Bruno in there getting something for the grill. He grabbed me by the arm as I was going to the bathroom and said, "I do not like that boy. There's something very bad about him that I don't like. He's no good for you. He's a shrimp and a loser. You don't need a low-life guy like that. Please get rid of him!"

How was it so obvious to everyone that Devin was bad news? He'd been polite and reserved the whole time and had worn a shirt with long sleeves so nobody could see what he had done to himself.

"Okay, don't worry. I'm planning on it. Please be patient," I said, reeling from his warning.

"Good. Get him out of here after you guys have finished eating. I cannot stand to look at him. I don't trust him."

When I returned outside he was looking very annoyed that I had left him for so long. I got up to get some food and pretended he wasn't there.

"Let's get out of here," he suddenly said, throwing his paper plate into the trash can.

I gave everyone a hug and said my goodbyes. Once I was inside his car he glared at me and chanted, "Jennifer, Jennifer, Jennifer," in a chilling way, like someone in a horror movie. "Your family doesn't like me at all. Your family's no good. They're all losers!" He was enraged at being rejected without them even trying to get to know him. I felt a little sorry for him because I knew what it was like to have everyone turn their back on you. I couldn't leave him just yet.

Chapter 23

Around the middle of July, my mother booked a flight for her, me and my best friend Eva to visit Gallaudet University, the only university in the world for deaf and hard of hearing students. Devin flew into a rage when I told him I was going to Washington D.C. and turned into that sinister movie character, repeating, "Jennifer ... Jennifer ... Jennifer ..." Then he said, "I know you're planning on leaving me just like my other bitch girlfriend."

"No, you're wrong," I reassured him. "I'm not leaving you. My parents will be suspicious if you don't let me go."

We left for Boston Airport at 5am. I felt so carefree being away from Devin without him spying on me like he did when I was at school. I wouldn't have to look over my shoulder once we were in Washington D.C.

Eva and I were crazy with excitement because we had an appointment for our tour of Gallaudet the next day. Our motel wasn't luxurious like the hotel we had stayed at in Washington D.C. before, but it had a swimming pool. After we had fooled around in the water, we showered, got dressed and walked to the little Irish restaurant down the street.

Inside it was dark and smelled of old beer. It was crammed with wooden tables and chairs and had green shamrock flags and Irish memorabilia everywhere. Behind the bar the entire back wall was covered from floor to the ceiling with lines of liquor bottles, which glistened under the dim lights. I ordered my favorite Rueben sandwich and French fries. I was so glad I wasn't with Devin. There was no question. I had to break up with him when I got home.

I looked over and I saw a handsome boy with blond hair sitting next to his younger brother, chatting with his parents. They weren't using sign language, so I guessed he was hearing. For some reason I couldn't take my eyes off him and he kept smiling back at me. His family kept looking over at us because we were all signing to each other.

I told Eva, "Wow that boy is so cute. I wish he was my boyfriend." We started laughing so hard.

My mother said, "What's so funny?"

I signed, "I really like that boy. He's so hot!"

My mom turned to look at him and signed to me, "Yes, you are right. He's a very handsome boy."

Throughout dinner Eva and I exchanged silent messages, while he stared at us, chewing his food and occasionally smiling. Every so often he would chat with his family. Suddenly he got up and walked over to our table. I signed quickly to Eva, "Oh my god, he's coming over."

He looked at me and said, "Hello," in sign language and finger spelled his name, "Matt." I wanted to hide under the table. He had understood everything I'd communicated to Eva and my mom. I blushed red as he explained, "I'm deaf too but I can speak very well." He was exactly like me and could hear with hearing aids and talk pretty well. I introduced him to my mom and Eva. Then his family came over and started to chat with my mother. They were here for a tour of Gallaudet just like us. Matt and I locked eyes and couldn't stop staring at each other.

"Where are you staying?" he asked, smiling. I told him the name of the hotel and he said, "Oh, we're directly across from you."

I said, "Why don't you meet me and Eva at the pool at our hotel tonight so we can hang out together."

He smiled and replied, "Sure." He left with his family while we were finishing up our desserts. Matt was perfect for me. He could talk like me and he was so handsome, and slightly taller than me.

Eva looked at me and said, "You'd better break up with that hearing guy."

"I know. I will break up with him by telling him in a nice way face to face rather than disappearing on him like his last girlfriend."

Matt brought his younger brother with him, which was smart because he kept Eva company while we got to know each other. He grabbed my waist, pulled me up close and put his lips on mine without stopping for air. I felt chemistry exploding everywhere inside me. I wanted him badly. I kissed his neck and I ran my hands through his thick, beautiful blond hair.

He said, "I love you."

"Me too," I replied breathlessly.

He looked at me and said, "Please go to Gallaudet. I'll meet you there and we can be a couple and help each other with homework and have a future together."

I couldn't wait to start this wonderful new part of my life, but there was just one niggling problem. How could I tell him I had a crazy, hearing boyfriend back home? I pretended he didn't exist. We said goodnight and I walked back to the motel. I opened the door and saw my mother sitting upright in bed reading a book.

"Thank god you're going to Gallaudet," she said. "Now you can get rid of that awful shrimp of a boyfriend. I'm so happy you met Matt. He seems like a very nice boy and he's so handsome. Did you know they live in Maine, which isn't far from Massachusetts?" I beamed at that thought of being with Matt forever. He was my first true love. Not a teenage crush. I had never felt such passion. Matt sure beat all of my previous dates and boyfriends.

We took a cab over to a beautiful campus, with lots of old castle-style buildings made from dirty white stone. There was a massive brick wall around the grounds to separate it from the bad neighborhood nearby. Many parents had already arrived with their grown-up kids and assembled in the hall. An official stood on the stage and told us in sign language what it meant to be at Gallaudet.

Matt squeezed my hand and said, "Let's meet tonight before you go home tomorrow."

"Yes of course. I'd love to see you. I'm sorry it will be our last time," I replied, tearing up a little.

We were shown the classrooms, cafeteria, dormitories and book store. I loved the grey Gallaudet sweatshirt with its dark-blue and yellow logo and the T-shirt in the same design. Mom bought them both for me. I pulled on Matt's hand and we fooled around, throwing stuff at each other in the campus store. He got the same sweatshirt and T-shirt to wear for when we were both at Gallaudet in the fall, after we'd both graduated high school. We promised each other we would write and call each other on TTY every day. Then we pinkie promised and crossed our hearts that we would meet again. I was heartbroken that I was going home and dreading breaking up with Devin.

That night we all met up for dinner at the same Irish restaurant. Matt and I just gazed at each other adoringly. Then we told everyone we were going for a walk. My mom looked at me, a little annoyed, and said, "Make sure you're back at the motel room by ten o'clock because we have to get up at five to go to the airport." A lead weight of sadness dropped into my stomach as I remembered my twisted life back home. Matt walked me away from his brother and Eva to take me somewhere private. We found a quiet dark corner near the pool and he hugged me tightly.

"I wish I wasn't going home," he said, grasping my hand.

"I wish we could run away together right now," I replied.

He kissed me passionately and we continued like this for hours, hardly talking, which was good because I might have confided in him about my situation. I felt sick at the thought of Devin. How was I going to break up with him without him going berserk? I was terrified of what he would do.

Matt had tears in his eyes when the time came to say goodbye. I turned around to walk away from him, and then I glanced back. He was watching me leave. I ran back to him, kissed him on his neck and cried on his shoulder. I didn't want to let go of him.

We returned to Boston Airport, where Eva's mother was waiting to pick her up and take her home. I was so nervous about going back to reality. When I got home my father was in the kitchen waiting for us.

"Guess who kept calling here every day? That boyfriend of yours. He called at all hours of the day demanding to know where you were, what hotel you were in and the phone number. 'Course I never told him. It's none of his business. The guy's unstable."

"I promise I'm going to break up with him soon. I just need time."

"You don't have to tell him you're breaking up with him. Just disappear. No words need to be said."

Later that evening I got a TTY call from Matt. I was ecstatic to hear from him. We chatted for hours. It drove my mom and dad crazy that we were on the phone so long because the TTY machine makes a loud clacking sound. As soon I hung up the phone it immediately rang again. My mother answered it. She told me it was Devin and he sounded angry. Then she said something quickly to him that I didn't understand and handed me the receiver. He was incandescent with rage.

"I've been trying to call you for hours and the line's always busy. Are you talking to another boy behind my back?"

"No, my father was on the phone for business."

"I want to see you this weekend. I've missed you. When can I see you?" I told him I'd see him on Saturday because I'd made plans with my friend on Friday night. He accused me of not wanting to see him and launched into another tirade. To this day I look back and wish I had taken my father's advice.

Chapter 24

Saturday came and I told my parents I was sleeping over at a friend's house. I didn't want them to know I was seeing Devin. I arrived at his house fully prepared to tell him that our relationship was over. He was in the driveway working on his bike. When he saw me he ran up and gave me a hug. But it wasn't like hugging my lovely tall Matt. It was different and I hated it. He suggested that we go for a walk in the park. I thought that would be the perfect time to tell him. We walked to a bench and sat down. I was very nervous and quiet.

"What's wrong?" he asked.

"Well, I don't know how to tell you this, but I want to break up with you. I'm really sorry."

His face got red and he shrieked manically, "WHY, WHY, WHY?" Then he said, "Jennifer ... Jennifer ... Jennifer ... Jennifer ..." in that deep, scary voice and fixed me with his dead eyes. "No. You are not breaking up with me."

"I don't have any feelings for you and you're too short for me. I really am sorry." He started to cry. I'd never seen a guy cry before. Tears were streaming down his face. "We can be friends. You can find someone else who's hearing and I can find someone else who's deaf," I reasoned.

He looked at me and shouted furiously, "NO! I want you and only you forever."

I implored, "But I can't be with you. You can't force me to stay with you. I hope you can understand. Please! Don't make this harder for me. We're not right for each other. Everyone says so."

"Who cares what other people think!" he raged. I walked back toward my car, with him following me. "I can drive you home. I have go back home to my family too," he said in a calm, reasonable voice. I was so relieved he had accepted it was over. All the time I had been thinking of Matt and I couldn't wait to get home to talk to him on TTY.

We parked on the driveway of his foster parents' house in Hyde Park. "Come to my room so I can give you back your things to take home," he said. I remembered that my make-up, my teddy bear and one of my sweaters was still in the bedroom of his basement apartment.

"Sure," I replied. I wanted my possessions back and then I'd never visit this place again. I stood near the door while he got my stuff from the other side of the queen-sized bed. He leaned down to get something from the floor. I thought he was picking up my clothes but he stood up holding a large black object and directed it right at me. I froze in horror. It was the worst shock I had ever felt in my life. It was an army-issue machine gun, like the ones you see in Vietnam War movies.

"Don't move an inch or I'll shoot you. Sit on the bed and stay there." I was shaking badly as I did as he said. Then he grabbed his desk chair and sat on it backwards with his gun just inches from my heart and his finger on the trigger. I wanted to get up and run away but I was pretty sure he would have shot me in the back. He glared at me with rage in his eyes, chanting, "Jennifer … Jennifer … Jennifer."

Then he came up close to my ear and screamed, "You're not breaking up with me! I know where you live. I know where your grandparents live and your uncle and your aunt. I know every last thing about your family. You'll be my girlfriend forever and if you disobey me I'll go after your family and friends and kill them all. I'll chop your brother into small pieces and put him in a garbage bag and hide it in the woods. Then I'll kill your friends at school. I know where you all sit in the cafeteria. And if you go to the police and report me they'll do nothing. You're not breaking up with me. I won't allow it."

He repeated, "Jennifer! Jennifer! Jennifer!" in his deep, creepy voice. I was crying and shaking and my heart was beating so fast. I knew he was right about the police. I'd seen a TV show where a woman told the police she was being abused and they only arrested him after she was dead.

"Please let me go home. My parents will be wondering where I am."

"No, you are staying here in my bed tonight. You're not going anywhere. My foster parents won't be home until the morning. You're all mine," he smirked.

I told him I had to use the bathroom, thinking I could make a run for it somehow.

"No! You can hold your piss."

Four hours went by and it was getting darker outside. His machine gun had been aimed at me the entire time. Then he got up and said, "I'll be right back." He needed to go to the bathroom and was testing me to see if I'd try to escape. I was so afraid of being shot that I remained motionless on the bed until he returned.

"I'll reward you with a trip to the bathroom for not moving but you have to come straight back. If you make a run for it I'll shoot your car and kill you instantly. I'll chase you on my motorcycle if I have to," he warned.

I went to the toilet. My hands were shaking so badly I could hardly hold the paper. When I was finished I walked slowly back into his bedroom. He had a different gun now, a black pistol. I sat back down on the bed.

"I've got even more guns stashed in my closet," he warned, smiling.

"Please can I smoke?" I needed an excuse to move a little because I was starting to get cramps from sitting so long in the same position. He gave me a cigarette. Now I was able to shift my arms and legs, which was a relief. After I'd finished with the cigarette he screamed into my face like a drill sergeant.

"I will kill you if you ever leave me! If you do one wrong move, I will kill your family. You know I'll do it." Then he growled, "Jennifer," over and over again. I was beginning to hate my name. He kept doing this every couple of hours.

"Oh yeah," he cackled, "And if I ever get put in jail, I won't be there for long. I'll come out meaner and madder and kill you and your whole family no matter what. You can't tell a soul about this, not even your close friends. Because you know they'll grass on you. And when they do, you can say goodbye to everyone you know."

I felt vomit rising up in my throat and told him I was going to throw up. He rushed to get me a bucket to puke into. I sat up straight in bed so I could reach it. All of sudden he pushed me down on the bed.

"Take your clothes off, now!" he demanded. "I want to see you naked."

"No! I don't want to take my clothes off."

He pressed the end of the gun barrel into my forehead. "Take your clothes off! You've got twenty seconds or I'll shoot you!" My fingers were shaking as I hurried to undo my jeans. He unzipped his pants and took his shirt off while holding the gun in his right hand. Then he got on top of me with the pistol pointed at my head.

"Open your legs now!" I felt his hard penis as he entered me forcibly. I was crying so hard as he tried to fuck me. "Shut up or I'll shoot you!" he ordered. Unable to hold the gun and perform, he put the weapon on the bed behind him. I wanted so badly to kick him off me and run to my car but he had hidden my keys. He was forcibly going in and out very hard. Then he grabbed my legs and put them over his shoulders and banged me until he came. I felt so dirty and wanted to throw up over him.

"Go to the bathroom," he instructed, prodding my butt towards the door with his gun. He watched me clean up with toilet paper and told me to put my clothes back on. I was quaking with terror.

"Get back and stay there on the bed. Hurry up! And don't you dare move!" I kept thinking of my loving parents, my safe house, my pink bedroom with my TV and my lovely Matt. At around eleven o'clock he was still sitting in his chair aiming his pistol at me. In those long hours my nerves settled enough for me to finally speak.

"You don't need to point that gun at me at me anymore. I'll do what you tell me do. I won't say anything about this. I promise."

"I don't trust you. I'm going to lie down and you'll lie next to me." I didn't want him touching me or raping me again, so I lay down flat on my back with my clothes on, staring at the ceiling. He turned to his side and pointed the gun at my head.

"Stop shaking or I'm going to have to shoot you."

I had to relax and think of something that made me happy, so I pictured Matt and I kissing each other at the motel and I finally calmed down. He dozed off, still gripping his gun. I wanted to escape but I was scared he would hear me and shoot me in the back. I had to survive this somehow. The red numbers on his digital alarm clock said 2.11am. That's the last thing I remember before I drifted off to sleep. A few hours later I was startled awake.

"Be quiet!" he commanded, putting his finger on my mouth. His foster parents Jim and Cathy were in the kitchen talking. I could see the shadows from their feet underneath the locked door. Devin got on top of me and put one hand on my mouth and held his pistol with the other. "Act normal. Get your make-up on and brush your hair. Treat me like I'm your boyfriend and pretend you care about me."

He finally let go of me and went to hide his guns. My face was a mess. My mascara was everywhere and my hair was matted and lank from sweat. There was a little bit of make-up in my purse so I tried to make myself look better, but my eyes were still puffy and bloodshot from crying all night. I went into the kitchen and sat down at the table and said hello. His foster parents looked at me and made some kind of joke together.

"Do you want eggs and bacon?" Jim asked.

"Sure, yes please. I'd love some breakfast." I was trying hard not to give them the impression their adopted son had just raped me and had threatened to kill me all night.

Then Cathy said, "Oh my goodness! Your eyes are so red. Are you okay?" I quickly explained that I had allergies and this always happened around this time of year. Devin stood in the corner monitoring our conversation and occasionally mouthing warnings.

"So what are you guys doing for Thanksgiving?" Devin asked.

"We're all going over to my sister Pam's house and you two lovebirds are invited," Jim replied cheerfully. "You'll have to meet Pam, her husband and their four children. They're a wonderful family to hang out with. We always have a great laugh, right?" he smiled, winking at Devin.

"Yes. Definitely," he replied. "They're the best. They make the best turkey, stuffing and mashed potatoes."

I felt sick. I didn't want to be with him or his family. I wanted to be with mine. I forced myself to smile and said, "I'd love to meet them." I got up after finishing eating my breakfast and told them I had to go home because my parents were expecting me. Jim and Cathy got up and hugged me.

"We are so happy to welcome you to our family. You're a very nice girl for Devin. We can see some positive changes in him already," Jim said.

Devin followed me to the car. There was a huge picture window from the kitchen looking out onto the driveway so he couldn't do anything violent in front of them. He put his head through my car window and said, "You're not going to Gallaudet University. You're going to live with me for the rest of your senior year. And answer the phone when I call or I'll come over and shoot you all."

He leaned over and kissed me on the mouth. I hated him touching me. I pulled out of the driveway and quickly sped up to the highway, crying uncontrollably. I could hardly see through the tears and I started shaking again. What am I going to do? Why me? I asked myself over and over. Not going to Gallaudet was the most distressing thing of all. Now I couldn't be with Matt. That love had been destroyed overnight. I had to protect him by pretending it was over between us.

When I arrived home, a huge yellow envelope was waiting for me on the kitchen counter. I opened it, sitting on my bedroom floor. It was a large photograph of Matt in his senior year, accompanied by the sweetest love letter. I broke down in floods of tears, hugging his picture and letter to me. I knew I would never see him again.

Chapter 25

I was fearful about going back to school with Devin's threats hanging over my head. He had repeatedly told me he would shoot any guy that talked to me. It was my senior year and it should have been the best year of my life, but it was all I could do to stop myself from bursting into tears. I wanted my old life back.

Devin told me there was a triple decker apartment in a three-story townhouse in Hyde Park. He said I had to move in with him or he'd come over and teach me a lesson. I was seventeen and could legally move out, but I didn't know how to tell my parents.

Kathy and Joseph waved to me to join them in the homeroom before I boarded the bus to Randolph High. They saw me standing there dressed all in black, looking like I'd been to a funeral.

"What's wrong?" they asked immediately. Deaf people can read body and facial expressions better than hearing people.

"Nothing's wrong. I'm just tired," I lied.

"You've lost weight and I've never seen you so sad," Joseph said, looking concerned.

I saw David and his usual crowd standing like seniors, tall and confident. I looked over my shoulder and checked the windows to make sure Devin wasn't there. I was petrified I'd get caught talking to them. The way he had forced himself onto me and his demands for oral sex, which I hated, with a gun pressed to my head, plagued my thoughts. He had forced his penis down my throat, which made me gag constantly. Then he told me how to suck it correctly until I gave him the perfect blow job. It had to be done to his exact specifications. He even grabbed my hair to force my head to go up and down at the right speed. When I didn't do it right he hit me in the head and screamed at me for vomiting over him.

"Hey, pay attention. You seem really spaced out and in dream land. Are you in love with your hearing boyfriend?" David said, nudging me in the ribs.

"Please stop mentioning him. I don't want to hear it," I begged.

"You don't love him," David replied. "I can tell."

"Shut up! Just shut up! I'm not in a good mood. Please leave me alone. I mean it. Leave me alone!"

I went to a desk at the back of the classroom and cried. Everyone looked at me with pity and confusion. After class David walked up to me and said, "What has happened to the old Jennifer I knew last year; the funny one who laughed all the time? Something's seriously wrong. Is your boyfriend hurting you?"

"Please, please just leave me alone," I replied. Then I ran to the bathroom and hid in a stall, crying uncontrollably. The homeroom teacher came after me and asked me what was wrong. I made up a story that I was upset because I'd been fighting with my parents, then I returned to the classroom. David tried to give me a hug but I pushed him away and checked the windows to see if Devin was watching. I didn't want to get David killed.

Mrs. Lindsey, our homeroom teacher, announced that we had to vote for Student Council this year. I was voted in as a representative and David was elected President of Senior Class, then we all went over to Randolph High. Ever mindful of Devin's promise to track my every move, I kept looking out in the hallways and behind the doors. I'm sure I saw his face briefly and felt like I was going to pass out. I was dreading going to the cafeteria because there were hundreds of students in there and it would be impossible for me to see him in the crowd. I was terrified that some boy would flirt with me and all of a sudden there would be a burst of gunfire.

At the end of the day I went to the parking lot. I was the only girl who drove to school and back every day, but my routine had changed now. Devin expected me to return to him immediately after school and had timed how long it took. He made me wear a watch at all times so there was no excuse for me being late.

Since leaving the psychiatric hospital I was still talking to a counselor once a week. She knew about my fake suicide attempt and that I had a new boyfriend who I had met at the facility. The counselor had researched Devin's history and was strongly advising me to break up with him, saying he was very volatile and unstable. One day I was sitting in her office when the door burst open wide. It was Devin. He had barged past the secretary in reception, who had tried to stop him entering. He looked at me and yelled, "Get up and get out of here. You're not coming back to counseling again. Do you hear me?"

The counselor stood in between us and said to him sternly, "You have no right to barge in and tell her what to do." Then she looked at me and said, "You mustn't go with him. I'm going to call the police right now." She rushed to the desk to pick up the phone.

Devin warned, "Remember what I said to you the other day?"

"It's okay. I'm fine. Please don't call the police. He's just upset that he thinks you're trying to break us up," I explained, adding, "I really do love him."

I knew he would kill everyone in sight if I didn't cooperate. I drove my car closely behind his and followed him to a store parking lot. I was upset that I would never see my counselor again. She knew sign language and I was comfortable with her. I should have signed to her that Devin was crazy and was keeping me imprisoned. But I didn't because the police wouldn't arrest him anyway. As far as everyone knew, I was his girlfriend and he hadn't hurt me in any way.

Chapter 26

Devin had instructed me to pick him up at Quincy Center Station because he was going drinking with his father in Boston and needed a ride home. He told me to pick him up at 5pm and to be there on time or he'd kill me. He also said that if he was late, I had to wait for him.

I showed up five minutes early and watched people swarm into the car park every fifteen minutes. I waited. It was after 5:30pm and he was nowhere in sight. Two hours later I decided to risk it and go home. As I was about to turn the key in the ignition I looked in my rearview mirror and saw Devin running towards the car with his pants halfway down his legs and his white underwear showing. His face was black with soot. He opened the passenger door and slumped forward into the passenger seat. I could smell alcohol and guessed he'd been drinking all day. But why were his pants all ripped up?

"Devin! Devin!" I said, patting his back trying to make him wake up. People were peering into the car to see what was wrong. They'd seen him lurching down the road in his shredded pants. I was so embarrassed to be with this loser. I quickly drove away and parked on a side street. I pushed his face up and saw his lips were blue and he wasn't breathing. I felt his neck for a pulse like I had been taught at school, but couldn't find one. He was dead in front of me.

I panicked. Should I just leave him like this or should I take him to hospital? I realized God was watching me and I would go to hell on Judgment Day if I didn't help him. But I wanted him to die so badly. Damn! I had to try to save him. I sped along the highway at over a hundred miles an hour to the emergency room, slammed on my brakes and yelled at the security guard that I had a person on my front seat who wasn't breathing. He got on his radio and within seconds a team of nurses and doctors ran out with a wheeled stretcher. They lifted him on and a nurse got on top of him and did CPR while the stretcher was pulled away.

Someone called my parents and told them to meet me at the hospital. They arrived an hour later. The nurse said, "It doesn't look good. He's in an induced coma right now. He was electrocuted by a train. A witness had called the police at the station after seeing him trying to climb over the fence to avoid paying his fare."

I thought, "Wow, and how stupid is that? He had money to pay for his beer and get drunk."

She said his alcohol level was way over the limit and had contributed to the fact that he had stopped breathing. Then she said, "There's a priest in there with him right now giving him his last rites."

"Let's go home," I said to my parents. "There's nothing we can do here." I prayed that he would die soon. I never wanted to see him again.

The next day I went to school as usual, thinking Devin was most likely gone forever. Then my mother got a phone call from the hospital. He had woken up and written a note, demanding to see me. I was so disappointed. How stupid was I to take him to the hospital?

I remembered his vile threats and went to see him after school the next day. He couldn't talk because of the tubes down his throat but he was raging and giving me the middle finger, 'Fuck you!' Then he pretended to shoot me. I turned around to leave, when suddenly I felt cold water splashing over my arms. He had thrown his plastic water pitcher at me. Then he ripped the IV line out of his arm and blood squirted everywhere. He yanked the plastic tube from his throat and started to come after me in his hospital gown, which was untied in the back. We ran past the ICU nurses' station and I dashed to the ladies bathroom and locked myself in.

He pounded on the door screaming, "You heartless bitch! I'm going to kill you!" I could hear people shouting and saw shadows moving under the door. I was too scared to open it and started to cry. Then everything went quiet. I heard a male nurse saying something I couldn't understand. He slid a note under the door, which said it was safe for me to come out. I opened up the door slowly and saw about five nurses and five policemen crowded around his bed across the hall, giving him shots and putting restraints on his feet and arms. Two male nurses and two cops were waiting for me when I came out crying and shaking. I was taken to another room.

The male nurse implored, "You have to leave him. He's mentally ill. You have to get far away from here and do not come back. Let us handle him. We'll have him transferred to a mental institution once he gets out of here. That buys you enough time to leave the state."

I went home and immediately asked my father if I could get a flight out to California to live with my aunt. I had to get away from Devin. I could go to the deaf high school and attend Northridge College over there. An hour later he said, "Your mother doesn't want to pay for the plane ticket. You have to stay here and face up to your problems. You created them, so you have to deal with them."

I was so upset. They had no idea of the danger I was in. I couldn't tell them or else they'd be shot. Thanks to my mom I had no choice but to stay where I was and pray that he wouldn't bother me again.

A few weeks later I went back to school. I had a feeling that something wasn't right. Devin was standing in the car park waiting for me. I felt sheer terror go through me.

"I'm back!" he said in a singsong voice. He slapped me across the face. Then he said "Jennifer," three times. "You're a bitch for leaving me at the hospital and not showing up when I needed you. I'm living in a halfway house in Whitman. You must visit me every single day without fail. And quit telling me you're breaking up with me. Are you out of your mind? You belong to me."

Chapter 27

Something was wrong with me. My boobs were hurting and I was so tired I'd sleep on the couch as soon as I got home from school. My mother knew right away I was pregnant because she recognized all the symptoms.

"You are pregnant aren't you?" she said. "I've been keeping track of your menstrual periods every month and I do not see any pads or tampons in the trash can lately."

Oh my god, who does that? Who keeps track of their own daughter's menstrual cycle? I thought to myself. I was disgusted that I could have gotten pregnant by Devin through forced horrible sex. I got a pregnancy test from CVS. Sure enough, it was positive. I was shocked and told my mother, who told my father when he got home from work. Both of them were devastated and insisted that I had to have an abortion to get rid of it. In the meantime, Devin kept calling my house and asking my parents where I was. My mother told him I was sick with flu and he couldn't visit. But when she went to work, I drove over to see him, because I feared he would show up at the house and kill us all.

I told him I was pregnant. He hollered with joy and jumped up and down. He wanted his brother Billy and his girlfriend Dottie to know because she had just found out she was pregnant almost at the same time as me. We went over and he proudly announced to the group, "Guess what? I'm having a baby!"

I was so confused. My parents wanted me to have an abortion but he wanted me to keep it. I couldn't be happy like he was. He would surely harm the baby with his guns and threats. There was no way I could let this child grow up with such a sick and terrifying father.

My mother had contacted an abortion clinic and told them I was more than two months along. They said I was cutting it very close to the deadline and had to go in on Monday and not a day later. The following day the phone rang almost continually, which annoyed my parents. I told them I had to see Devin but they took away my car keys. The phone kept ringing. Finally Mom took his call and screamed, "She's having the abortion on Monday. Leave us alone! Don't you dare come over here! Stop calling! She's not going to talk to you!" She took the receiver off the hook. I panicked and ran to my room and locked the door. I spent the next few hours nervously peering out of the window to see if he was outside watching the house from his car. I was so relieved that we all made it through to Monday alive without incident.

My mother drove me over to a clinic in Boston. It was stressful, wondering what I was about to go through, as nobody had explained anything to me. There were no sign language interpreters so I was lost in all of this process. There were a lot of girls around my age and some older women in the waiting room.

Some had their partners for support, some were alone, and some were accompanied by their mother or a friend.

A nurse came up to me with a plastic cup and said, "Here, take this pill and drink some water with it."

All of sudden I was having second thoughts. I didn't want to kill my baby but my mother kept pushing me to get it over with, saying, "This will bring shame on our family and embarrassment to our friends. Swallow the pill and you can get on with your life without being tied to a baby from a boyfriend who's no good for you."

Feeling under pressure to do as she asked, I took the pill and sat there quietly, thinking about the little life inside me that was being slowly poisoned to death. About an hour later the nurse said, "Are you ready to go up in the elevator?" I was taken to a sterile room on the 4th floor. There was a huge machine in there with a vacuum hose attached to it.

"Don't worry, it will be over soon. You are doing the right thing because you're too young to be pregnant," the nurse said, smiling.

I was shocked to discover that I would be awake for the whole procedure and wasn't going to be given anything to put me to sleep. Everyone had blue masks on and I had no clue what they were talking about. Then a doctor came into the room quickly, shoved the vacuum hose into my vagina and turned the machine on. I felt pulling and tugging and watched as a load of blood and gunk was sucked up the clear plastic hose. I started to sob uncontrollably. I was so mad at myself for getting rid of my baby and regretted it immediately. The doctor quickly left the room to remove another dead fetus. This is what he did all day long. The nurse told me go into the bathroom to put a thick pad in my underwear and then go to the lounge to sit in a recliner. There were five other girls in there, resting like me, but I was the only one crying. They all looked happy their ordeal was over.

We drove in silence all the way home and my mother never said a word about what had happened from that day on. My father brought me my favorite McDonalds Big Mac and fries because he felt bad about what I'd been through. The only good thing to come out of this was I had stopped hearing from Devin for a while. My mother had warned him to stay away from us and I believed that he had finally stopped terrorizing me.

For the first time in weeks I slept soundly.

Chapter 28

About a week after my abortion I was beginning to settle into my new life of freedom, confident that Devin would never bother me again. I arrived home at around 2pm because it was early release day and I went upstairs to freshen up. As I was brushing my hair in my bathroom, the shower curtain ripped open and Devin leapt out. He grabbed me by my neck, slammed my head hard onto the side of the tub and tried to choke me. His hands were gripped around my throat and he was twisting his arms, trying to break my neck. I tried to pry his fingers away but they wouldn't move. He was too strong for me. I could feel my lungs tightening and the pressure building behind my eyes. I had to think of something to save my life.

I reached out with my hands and spelled, "I love you," in sign language to his face. Suddenly he let go. "Please don't kill me. I promise I will do anything you tell me. Please don't kill me," I begged, gasping for air.

"Jennifer … Jennifer … Jennifer …" he snarled, with a menacing look in his eyes. "You murdered my baby. How could you kill my baby?!"

"I'm sorry! I was confused. I was pressured into it by my parents. I wanted to keep it but they forced me get an abortion. I am so sorry," I sobbed, rubbing my neck.

"I should cut up your brother, put the pieces in a trash bag and throw it in the pond behind this house so your parents get to feel what it's like when their child is murdered like my mine was."

"Oh god, no! Please don't touch Antonio. I promise I'll treat you like you're my boyfriend again. Please forgive me. I love you very much."

"Okay. You'd better show up at my house tomorrow after school and you better not tell anyone what happened here or, seriously, I will kill your brother. Tell your parents you're moving out to live with me. If you don't, I'll kill everyone in your family, including you."

After he was gone I went to my room, threw myself on the bed and wailed into my pillow. My living hell was back again. After school the next day, I drove over to his place and found him sitting on the steps at the end of the driveway waiting for me. I felt disgusted. I didn't want to go near him.

"How was school today?" he asked, smiling. "Did you talk to any boys I don't know of?"

"No! I didn't talk to anyone today."

"That's bullshit!" he screeched. "I saw you with them! What about that dark-skinned Arab boy you were talking to this morning? I watched everything you did." I was horrified that he'd managed to get into my school and spy on me and David without anyone noticing.

"He's just a friend of mine. He needed to ask me about Student Council issues. He's harmless."

He slapped my face and said, "You'd better not be messing with me. I'm watching you." Then he grasped me by the wrist, pulling me so hard I could feel the tendons crunch, and he yanked me inside the house and into his bedroom.

"Take off your clothes and get on the bed right now."

"No. I can't. The doctor said it's dangerous!"

Quick as a flash he grabbed his gun from his closet. "Do what I say or I'll shoot you." We were back to this unbearable game.

"Please put that thing away," I begged. "I'll do anything you tell me to do."

He got on top of me and entered me forcefully, while holding his .45 pistol to my head. I couldn't wait for it to be over. I closed my eyes and tried to imagine I was with someone else, praying it would be over quickly. After a couple of minutes he was done. I didn't want to lie there next to him so I said I had to go to the bathroom. He gave me permission to use the one down the hallway. I wiped myself clean with hot water, doing my best to try not to get pregnant again, because he refused to use a condom. I kept wiping harder because I didn't want his bodily fluids inside me. Then I vomited in the toilet.

How could I escape from him? If I went to the police would they protect everyone that I knew? Could they arrest him for his threats? Devin had repeatedly told me they would do nothing because I wasn't rich or famous. I rushed back to his room and saw that he was already dressed.

"Let's go over to my friend Tony's place before my foster parents come home," he said.

"Okay. I'd like that," I replied, keeping my promise to agree to all his demands.

I got into his ugly beat-up car and we headed over to Tony's. I gazed out the window as we went down a busy pedestrian street. All of sudden I felt a punch to my nose so hard that it made my head spin to the right. It was so painful and blood started to trickle down onto my mouth.

"Why the fuck are you looking at those guys!" he screamed. I took a leftover McDonalds napkin from the floor and wiped my nose and looked straight ahead for the rest of the journey.

We went straight into Tony's living room without knocking, because the door was always open. Tony and Crazy Nick were sitting on the couch smoking weed. Tony passed his joint to Devin. They all looked at me, trying to work out what was wrong with my face. My nose was swollen and blocked with dried blood.

"Go on, try it," Devin said, handing me this stub of brown paper. "Inhale it deep and hold it for a few seconds. Then breathe out." It burnt my lungs in an unexpected way. Then all of sudden I felt high for the first time in my life. That little hit of weed changed my mood. I couldn't even believe how happy I was! Then Devin told me we were moving out of his parents' house and into the triple decker apartment in Billy and Dottie's house in Hyde Park.

"I can't!" I objected. "My parents will never allow it because I'm still in high school and I graduate this year!" I was in tears. I didn't want to leave my family and be with him every night. How could I even go to school? I knew my parents wouldn't let me keep my car.

"You can use my car to drive to school," he smiled, reading my mind.

When I went to the bathroom to pee I immediately felt a burning pain and even though no urine was coming out, it felt like I wanted to pee some more. The pain got worse and it was uncomfortable to sit down. I needed to go to a walk-in clinic or hospital.

Devin was angry. "Get in the car!" he shouted. "They'd better not bust you for smoking weed and find it in your blood." He dropped me off at the emergency room. I gave them a urine sample and sat for ages in the waiting room while he went back to see his friends. Then a nurse took me into a side room and confirmed that I had urinary tract infection. The doctor came in and wrote me a prescription for antibiotics.

"Have you had sex recently?" he asked bluntly.

"Yes," I replied, feeling ashamed.

"Well, this infection could be from sex with someone who isn't clean. You have to go to the bathroom to wash or preferably take a bath right away after sex."

"But I do that all the time," I told him. But it made no difference. I'd get this infection almost every time he forced himself onto me.

"Okay, well you mustn't have sex for two weeks, to allow yourself to heal, or your partner will become infected too." I asked the doctor to write that down so I could show Devin.

Then Devin came into my room. There were curtains around it and I had an IV in my arm to give me fluids because the doctor said I was dehydrated. Devin was annoyed and said, "This is taking too long. Let's get out of here now."

The nurse ran in and said, "She needs to finish the IV before she can be released."

"Fuck off. She's leaving right now!"

"I'm calling security!" The nurse ran off. Devin came over to my bed and yanked the IV needle out of my arm. Blood splattered across the white sheets and the floor.

"Get your clothes on now and take the prescription with you." He pulled me off down the corridor and made me run with him to the parking lot. Then he put his foot down and raced off before the security guard could catch us. It was just another day of drama, shame and terror at the hands of a madman.

Chapter 29

Knowing how reckless he was on his motorcycle, I was hesitant when Devin asked me to ride on the back of his bike all the way to Boston. He wanted to take me to a restaurant over there.

"You ready to ride with me to get a bite to eat?" he said, handing me a helmet.

"Yes, I'm ready, but please can you drive slowly and don't speed?"

"Get on, and be careful of that hot muffler," he warned. But I didn't hear him and my bare calf touched it, burning my skin. I screamed in pain.

"What did I say, you idiot! Be careful of that, it's hot!" he shouted.

"I'm deaf! I couldn't see what you said with your helmet on. I have told you millions of times, I can't hear when your back is turned!" I yelled back.

He started up the engine and zoomed off down the road, braking hard and swerving from left to right. After a couple of minutes he pulled over and yelled, "You're doing it all wrong. You have to lean in the same way I do when I turn a corner. You can't sit up straight." He slapped my leg.

"Okay! Stop it! I'll do it. You don't have to hurt me."

The next time he went around a bend I leaned my body in the same direction and my knee almost scraped the road. He gave me the thumbs up. Hurtling down the road to the highway I could hardly catch my breath I was so scared. I kept closing my eyes and praying we wouldn't crash. He kept slapping my leg to remind me to lean in, so I had to keep my eyes open to anticipate the turns. We were overtaking just about every car ahead of us.

Sweating and dry mouthed with fear, I got off the bike and shakily took my first steps on firm ground. We had arrived at a seafood restaurant in Boston Harbor. He ordered two plates of fried clams with fries and coleslaw and I sat and ate them, looking at the ocean. With any other boyfriend this would have been a nice date.

I noticed other couples sitting next to each other, all cozied up. They looked so normal, with the right height difference, and the guys were respectful and well mannered. I felt a pang of jealousy because I was stuck with this psychotic dwarf. We looked ridiculous together. After we finished eating he tried to kiss me but I looked away before his mouth met mine.

"Okay, let's go now," he growled. I got on behind him and he took off, spinning the wheels and leaving a cloud of exhaust fumes and the smell of burning rubber in our wake. The diners on the restaurant patio turned to stare at us. I thanked God I had a helmet to cover my face because I was so humiliated.

Going back he was even more reckless than before, speeding at more than 120mph. I kept glancing to the side of the road, hoping to see a highway patrol car. Then I noticed two eighteen-wheeler trucks up ahead, traveling at almost the same speed side by side. The one in the left lane was refusing to let the other one pass. Every time it tried to get ahead slightly, the other truck would speed up. They were locked together like two giant elephants. Devin was getting more and more infuriated that the truck in the right-hand lane wouldn't get out of his way. Suddenly he hit the throttle and rode down the gap between the trucks at 125mph.

"No! No! No!" I yelled. I was mad and terrified at the same time. I started hitting his back with my hand. Devin gripped the handles and kept his arms locked firmly in position. The trucks moved closer together on purpose to freak us out.

I was crying when we finally made it out alive. Devin pulled off at the next exit and stopped at the side of the curb. I jumped off the bike and screamed, "I don't care if you kill me right now. I'll never ride with you again! I don't care if you shoot me. It's better than being smashed up on the highway. I can't do this anymore!"

"Don't worry," he replied. "I'm never riding with you again either."

This was the first time I had spoken up against him and risked him shooting me.

"I am walking back to the house," I told him.

"Just remember, I know where everyone lives and you'd better come back and see me."

I walked along the side of highway for four hours to reach my car. Devin kept circling me on his motorcycle to check on me but I ignored him. It was the first time I had stood up to him. But what price was I going to pay for stepping out of line? What other horrors could he possibly have in store for me?

Chapter 30

Devin was keen for me to tell my parents about 'our' plan to live together. So I decided to tell them at the dinner table.

"Mom, Dad," I said nervously, "I'm leaving home. I'm old enough to make that decision. There's nothing you can say that will make me change my mind."

My mother burst into tears. "But what about Gallaudet University?"

"I can't go there."

"You're wasting your life! You're making a huge mistake choosing that loser over your future! He's no good for you! Can't you see that?" she cried.

"Please leave me alone and don't ask me any questions," I replied, looking down. I couldn't bear to see the anguish on their faces.

"How can you throw away the scholarship money? You got into that college for free with a grant and now you don't want to go?" my dad said, not believing what he was hearing.

"You'll never have a good life without a college education. You'll only be able to get low-paid jobs. You're wasting your life away with that awful boy!" Mom continued.

I couldn't stay there and listen to them so I started to go upstairs. They had no idea I was trying to save their lives.

"You're not taking the car and don't ask me for any money. You'll have to find a way to get to school on your own!" my dad yelled after me.

"Fine, I'll do it without your help," I yelled back.

As I was approaching the back door with my bags, my father threw me to the floor and held me down to stop me leaving. "You can't go! You are making a huge mistake!"

"Get off her! Let her go!" my mom yelled. "She's old enough to make her own choices. If she wants to ruin her life, let her. Let her learn the hard way."

The room at Billy and Dottie's house wasn't empty so we stayed at his foster parents' house temporarily. During this time Devin took me to a sex store in Boston because he wanted me to get an outfit to wear for him in bed. He picked out some white lingerie, with white stockings, suspenders and a pair of white high heels to match. He also bought the set in red and black, paying with a bad check like he always did. Then we drove over to Tony's place to hang out. Tony, Crazy Nick and older brother Ronnie were taking a break from fixing their old Mustang and were passing around a joint, drinking beer and laughing about something. I sat on Tony's beaten-up couch and watched TV. Then Devin came rushing in with the bag from the sex store.

"Put it on now and put on a show on for me and my buddies. I want them to see how sexy you are."

"No. I'm not doing it!"

Devin took me into the kitchen and said, "Do it now or I'll beat you to a pulp. Then I'll shoot you."

I put the lingerie on in the bathroom, taking my time, hoping Devin would forget, but of course he didn't. He opened the bathroom door and asked, "Are you ready yet?" When I emerged everyone was sitting down waiting for me. I was so nervous my whole body was trembling. They sniggered as I paraded myself in front of them, walking in circles and posing in front of the TV.

"Okay. Now take it off slow and sexy like a stripper," Devin commanded.

"Hey, chill bro', she doesn't have to strip for us," Ronnie said, seeing how uncomfortable I was. He exchanged harsh words with Devin and they almost got into a fight. While they were arguing I snuck off back to the bathroom and got changed. By the time I returned they had all gone outside to work on the car, so I sat down on the couch to watch TV.

Soon afterwards two girls came in and plopped themselves down on the loveseat at the side of my couch. One was pretty, with a sweet, innocent face. She had very short brown hair and wore beautiful make-up. It looked like her hair was in a ponytail, but she had just greased it back so it was flat against her head. The other girl, who was a little chubby, had long wavy blond hair.

"Hey, what's your name?" the pretty girl asked. I told them my name and she said, "I'm Vicki and this is my older sister Tracey. I'm dating Nick so we just came over to hang out. Who are you with?" she asked. I told her. She looked me up and down and said, "You're a beautiful girl. Why are you with him? I heard he's nuts and tried to kill himself by cutting his arms. You can do better than him."

I looked at her and said, "And you can do better than that too."

She laughed and said, "Nick treats me like a queen. He is really good to me."

"What do you want to do in the future?" I asked, curious as to whether she knew.

"I just graduated high school and want to go to paramedic school to be a first responder. That's my dream. But my Nick told me to wait and to focus on our relationship."

"Oh, that's too bad because you would have been finished by now and working as a paramedic."

"I know," she said sadly. "I really want to go to school and do it."

"Well you can. Don't let Nick tell you what to do."

Her sister said, "Yes, you should go for it. Look, I messed up my life by getting pregnant. Now I have two kids at home. I screwed my life up for a guy that's in jail for robbery."

Devin came in from the kitchen and joined us in the living room. He looked around and said, "What are you talking about?"

Vicki gave him a nasty look and said, "Go back outside. It's none of your business."

"Hey bitch! What were you talking about behind my back? Are you telling her I'm not good enough for her?"

"No! We are talking about me being a paramedic," Vicki replied.

He let out a whoop of laughter and said, "You will never become a paramedic. You're just white trash." He turned around and went back through the kitchen to the garage to be with his buddies.

"What an asshole," Vicki said.

I really wanted to tell her about his threats, but if I did I knew it would get all of us killed.

Chapter 31

Almost every day for the next few weeks we went to hang out at Tony's place. Devin preferred it there because he said his foster parents watched every move he made. Tony was in his thirties and had inherited his house from his parents who had passed away years ago. He owned the garage next door and fixed cars for a living.

Vicki's sister Tracey lived with him and he doted on her. I knew Tracey was an unfit mother who neglected her two little ones. They were always in heavy, soaked diapers and were never bathed. All she cared about was watching TV and chain smoking until Tony had finished work so they could go to his bedroom and have sex.

Crazy Nick lived with his older brother Ronnie in an apartment right behind Tony's small house. One day Devin said, "Let's surprise Crazy Nick and his girlfriend Vicki. It'll be a bit of fun." The door to their apartment was unlocked. Devin heard something and put his hand over my mouth and said, "Shhh … quiet."

We heard a scream coming from the bedroom. I looked at him and said, "What's going on?" Devin flung the bedroom door open. Crazy Nick was on top of Vicki, slapping her face hard repeatedly. She was half naked with her shirt ripped to her belly and her pants halfway down. He was holding her down and hitting her while she was screaming and crying.

Crazy Nick looked at Devin and said, "Come on in and take a look at this white trash bitch. She bit my mouth. This is all her fault."

I tried to turn and leave but Devin grabbed my wrist and said, "You're staying exactly where you are. You're going to watch this because if you cross me the same thing will happen to you."

I was shaking in horror as I was watched Crazy Nick brutalize her on the bed. She kept looking over at me asking for help. I froze because I was frightened that Devin would pull his gun out. But I couldn't just stand there so I took a chance and bolted out of my chair. I pushed Crazy Nick off the bed and yelled to Vicki, "Run! Run! Get out of here and never come back." Vicki got off the bed, pulled her pants up and grabbed her bag. But Devin shut the door.

"You fucking stupid bitch! I'm going to kill you right now!" Crazy Nick screamed.

Devin had one hand on the door and one hand on Nick's throat, warning, "No, you asshole. You're not touching her." Then he opened the door and told me to get out. I didn't know where to go because Devin had my car keys. I ran out onto the street and looked for Vicki. I could see her sprinting through Tony's yard.

She turned around and saw me. "Thank you!" she yelled. Then she got in the car and drove off. I had no idea where to go. Then I remembered Crazy Nick's mother lived across the street. She was always in her living room, smoking. I was crying when I reached her front door.

"Please can I come in? I'm too scared to be outside." I couldn't tell her what had happened. I sat in her living room and looked through the window across the street. Crazy Nick wouldn't dare to do anything to me in front of his mother. She was a tough old bird and smacked his head when he was out of line. Suddenly I saw both of them running towards the house. I braced myself for the worst. Crazy Nick and Devin stormed into the living room.

"Tell that bitch to get out of my house right now," Crazy Nick demanded, pointing at me.

"You better go with your boyfriend and give my Nick some space," his mother said. Devin motioned me to join him. I was terrified at what was in store for me. As I sat down in his car he punched me hard and sharp in the nose twice. Then he continued to beat me on my head and my back.

"You dumb bitch!" he screamed. "You did the stupidest thing ever! What the fuck were you thinking? You're lucky to be alive."

I was sobbing hysterically. The horror show scene of Crazy Nick punching Vicki played on a loop in my head. The irony was, I was watching myself. He did the exact same thing to me. There was blood all over my shirt from my nose. I knew it was broken and I wanted to go to the emergency room but he wouldn't take me.

"Wipe that shit up," he said, handing me some McDonald's napkins. "This is your own fucking fault."

Chapter 32

In the fall, around mid-October, I moved into the Hyde Park apartment in Billy's house. I packed as much as I could fit into Devin's beat-up Torino. We arrived at the tall three-story house. There was no elevator and the apartment was on the top floor. I had to carry everything in on my own as none of his roommates volunteered to help.

Devin had got a full-time job working overnight at a local gas station, pumping gas. He was also dealing cocaine for a small mafia group south of Boston. Every morning I'd go to school in his car and he'd sleep through the day while I was doing my lessons. There was no way for him to check on me unless he borrowed a car from a friend.

We slept on a mattress on the floor and used cardboard boxes as bedside tables. I felt really poor for the first time in my life. I'd had such a comfortable childhood. Now here I was in this ghetto neighborhood, scraping by on a few dollars a day.

One evening, while Devin was at work and I was in the bedroom, Billy's girlfriend Dottie knocked at my door. "You should join us in the living room," she grinned. "We've got some VHS tapes from the porn store and we're having a little party over at our place."

I recalled Devin's instructions to stay in my room and not to talk to anyone or he would torture me before shooting my brains out. I said, "Sorry, I can't. Devin won't let me." She laughed and called out to Billy a few times. Billy, Ronnie and Crazy Nick came to my bedroom door. I told them Devin would get mad if I joined them. So Crazy Nick said he'd call to ask Devin for permission. I had no idea that he was pretending to speak to him. Being deaf I wouldn't know he was talking into a dead phone.

"Okay, okay, you got it," Crazy Nick said. He hung up and smiled. "He said yes."

I sat in a plush chair near the door that came in from the hallway. There were about seven of us in the living room. Everyone was sharing a joint and sniffing white powder off a small mirror using a rolled up dollar bill.

"What's that?" I asked naively. They squealed with laugher.

"Oh my god, Jennifer doesn't know what this is!"

They looked at me wide-eyed in disbelief and said, "That's coke."

Billy, Crazy Nick and two other guys egged me on to try it. I was scared because I remembered the school lectures about staying away from drugs. I had never watched porn in my life and was shocked to see naked women and multiple guys having sex. Dottie looked at me, laughing, and said, "It's an orgy." Then she nudged me and said, "Come on, you have to try coke. We want to see your reaction."

She rolled up a dollar bill to use to snort the white powder up my nose, saying, "Just press on the other nostril with one finger and sniff it hard."

I felt very weird. I was super high but wide awake and very talkative. I wanted to go out dancing. I had enough energy to run to Boston and back. Everyone thought it was hilarious. I just wanted to leave and hit the dance floor.

"Seriously honey," Dottie said. "We can't go dancing right now because it costs money to get in. But we can dance right here." So I started to dance with Dottie and her friend Betty. All four guys were watching us and laughing.

The phone rang and Nick picked it up. He looked at me and said, "This is for you."

I took the receiver, telling him, "You know I can't hear too good on the phone." I could hear Devin screaming at me but I couldn't understand a word he was saying. I yelled, "It's okay! I'm having a wonderful time and I am dancing right now!"

I handed the receiver back to Crazy Nick, who started laughing uncontrollably. Then he got a little mad and threw the receiver on the floor after listening to it for a while. "He wants you to go back to your bedroom and stay there," he said.

"No!" I replied. "I'm having a good time dancing and I need some more coke." I snorted another line and felt so good. I forgot where I was and even forgot about Devin. I was so happy, jumping around in front of the TV. It was still showing porn but I didn't care.

About twenty minutes later the living room door slammed against the wall. Devin marched up to me and punched me in the eye. I fell backwards onto the floor. Billy, Ronnie and Crazy Nick pulled him off me and pushed him down the hallway. Then Billy hauled him up and threw him down the stairs. He went rolling and tumbling down to the next landing. Dottie was yelling at Devin and calling him names for punching me. She helped me to my feet and took me to the kitchen so she could put ice on the egg-sized bruise. I could hear him calling me a slut, a whore and all kinds of names from the hallway.

Ronnie was a huge guy. He got on top of Devin and told him to calm down. He said that I was innocent and all this was their fault. Devin got his gun out and pointed it at his own head. Billy screamed at him, "Yeh! Go right ahead and kill yourself. Do you want me to help?"

Finally Devin calmed down. He came to see me in the bedroom and shut the door. I was sitting on the bed crying. He looked at me sympathetically and said he was sorry. He said he got angry because he didn't want any guys to touch me and I wasn't allowed to have fun while he was working.

"But I got your permission from work. Nick called you to ask if it was okay."

He yelled, "I never got the call from Nick! He tricked you!"

I tried hard to calm him down, saying, "I promise I won't ever do it again."

"You have school tomorrow and you're high on coke. I never gave you permission to do coke without me. I use it all the time."

That night I was wide awake the entire time until morning, when I had to go to my class. I couldn't believe cocaine kept you awake for this long. In the early hours of the morning Devin pulled me over to him and said, "Give me a blow job, right now." He grabbed my hair and forcibly shoved my mouth onto his penis. I tried to do it perfectly, like he had taught me, to get it over with, but I didn't get it right. He yelled at me to press my tongue harder. I did as I was told and he finally came in my mouth. It tasted awful and I threw up in the toilet as soon he left for work.

I was running late for school and had to hurry because the school officials had warned me that if I kept showing up late they wouldn't let me graduate with the class next spring because I'd had too many tardies and absences. I got in the car, put my foot on the gas and drove at more than 80mph to Boston School. I arrived in the nick of time but the director of the school was standing outside. When she saw me she shook her head. My nose was still swollen and there were black bruises under my eyes.

"I had an accident and bumped into some furniture," I shouted, running past her to my homeroom before the bell rang. Everyone stared at me in horror.

"What the heck happened to you?" they asked.

"Yeh, whatever. I fell over and hit my face while I was moving furniture."

They sniggered and said, "Looks like someone punched you."

David looked at me suspiciously. "Where's your car?" he asked.

"I moved in with my boyfriend and I'm using his."

"Are you sure you are doing the right thing?"

"Yes, please don't worry."

He looked me in the eye and said, "I don't believe you. I think he's beating you. You have to leave him!" I knew that deaf people had a gift for reading people's facial expressions. There was no way I could deny what had happened to me. So I turned away to avoid his gaze.

All day long everyone kept asking, "What's happened to your face?"

I took the commuter bus over to Randolph High with Kathy and Joseph. They kept nudging me until I finally told them the truth. "Yeah, he hit me."

They both gasped and said, "You gotta leave him! He's going to hurt you badly." I knew it was true.

Chapter 33

As always, the boys were waiting for me in the hallway outside my classroom. I forced myself to smile but it was almost impossible because all the energy and life had been sucked out of me. Living in that dump with that monster had worn me down into a state permanent anxiety and depression. I walked to my desk, sat down and looked out of the window to check I wasn't being watched. Then I went back to Boston School to eat at their cafeteria because they were having an event for the whole school. Sean, one of the twins, stood in line behind me. He nudged me in the back and a group of his friends started laughing.

"What do you want?" I snapped.

"Did you know you're so freaking ugly? How do you ever get boyfriends looking like that?"

"Stop!" I begged and broke down in tears.

"Wow, I'm sorry," he said, shocked at my reaction. "I was just teasing you."

"No! I know you're serious about me being ugly."

All the emotions that had been building inside about my situation with Devin poured out of me. Sean and the others tried to calm me down and held me, saying, "It's okay. Please don't cry."

After dinner we went back to the homerooms to have our photos taken for the school yearbook. I went to the bathroom and plastered some foundation around my eye. I looked so tired. I was going to be featured in the yearbook in a group shot as a member of the Student Council. David tried to cheer me up but I couldn't handle any more attention.

"Stop calling me names and bullying me! I'm sick of you all," I screamed, and moved my desk to the back of the room. Everyone was stunned I was behaving this way. It wasn't me at all. The photographer asked us all to gather together but I refused and stayed at my desk in the corner. Then David and Sean marched over and pushed me in my chair with my desk attached like I was in a wheelchair and made me join the group. The photographer kept asking me to smile but I refused. I still have that picture in my yearbook, looking miserable.

Devin was waiting for me on the front steps of the apartment building with his group of friends when I got back to Hyde Park. As soon as I saw him I broke down crying and I ran upstairs to the bedroom. He chased after me and grabbed me by the shoulders.

"What's wrong?" he demanded. I didn't want to tell him because I didn't want to make everything worse but he insisted on knowing what had happened.

"I just had a really bad day at school. Just forget it."

He slapped me across the face and said, "You have to tell me everything in detail. I need to know what's going on."

"No. Just leave me alone. I've got tons of homework to do and I'm behind."

He punched me in the nose again. I got my handheld mirror to see if it was bleeding. It wasn't, but it hurt badly. He kept yelling at me to tell him what had happened.

"Jennifer … Jennifer … Jennifer … Jennifer …" he repeated menacingly.

Finally I told him Sean had called me names and said I was ugly. He instantly turned cold and calm. "No one talks to my girl like that. He's dead meat. Where is he? How do I find him?"

"No," I pleaded. "You're not going to touch him!" He pushed me to the floor, opened the door and yelled out of the window for his buddies to come upstairs. I was so scared I thought my heart was going to drop to the floor. How could I stop them from killing Sean? "Don't do anything to Sean please!" I implored him, crawling across the floor and begging on my knees. Ronnie, Crazy Nick and Tony were in the living room. Devin explained to them what had happened.

He looked at me and demanded, "Where are they? Are they at the school right now?" Tell me where they are or I'll kill you too." He got on top of me and tried to choke me. Ronnie grabbed him from behind and tried to pull him off. He kept yelling, "Where are they?" I told him they were playing basketball in the gym after school and he let go. Then he punched me in my leg very hard.

Ronnie kept trying to grab his arms, shouting "Enough!" I cried and begged him not to go over to the school.

He looked at me with a murderous glare and said, "What does he look like? Tell me!"

"He's about five feet seven inches tall with short blond hair and blue eyes, medium build. He was wearing jeans and a white turtleneck today. His basketball practice should be finished around six. It depends if they shower or not." In truth, I had no idea about their schedule and prayed he wouldn't find them.

Devin got his pistol and put it in his back pocket. I grabbed his leg as he was leaving and held it for as long as I could. He kept kicking it to get me off and smacking me on the head. Before he went downstairs he looked at me and said, "I'm going to kill Sean and all his buddies." He yelled at Dottie to watch me and make sure I didn't call the police.

I was sobbing on the floor near the apartment door as I watched them scrambling down the stairs. I shrieked, "No!" and ran to the living room window. He looked up and I saw a look of vengeance on his face. "No! No! No!" I gasped and I ran to the phone on the wall in the kitchen. Dottie grabbed it out of my hand. But who was I going to call? I didn't have Boston School's number and in those days the only way to find someone's number was from a phone directory. I was running in circles, crying. I had to go after them and warn Sean.

Crazy Nick's mother! She could drive me there. I ran across street and knocked on her door. "Please can I borrow your car to go somewhere?"

"Sorry hun, the tank is empty and I don't have any money for gas. And anyways I wouldn't let you drive it, 'cos it's my car, not yours."

"Never mind," I said, and ran back to my apartment. I was out of options, so I decided to pray by the window. I felt sick to my stomach and ran to the bathroom. Anything I ate went right through me because I was so distraught. All I could do was wait until they came back or I saw something on the news.

"Calm down," Dottie kept saying. "I'm sure they don't want to go to jail for this. They won't kill anyone."

Hours later, around 9pm, Devin's car pulled up. He was carrying a brown paper bag full of beer. The door opened and he laughed, "Yeh! I killed him. I saw these nerds using that weird hand sign language and went up to one of them and said, 'Are you Sean?' He said he was. I told him I was your boyfriend, and said, 'Did you call Jennifer ugly?' The guy said he was fooling around so I got my gun, stuck it in his belly and said, 'Don't ever say shit like that again or I'll kill you.'" Devin roared with laughter. "You should have seen his face! He looked like he was going to crap his pants!"

Oh my god, this was so awful. I couldn't go to school and face Sean after this. Now everyone would know what a nut job Devin was. But I'd had so many warnings that I wouldn't graduate if I missed any more days so I had to go.

Billy came home from work, looking confused and asking what the fuss was about. Dottie explained everything to him in the kitchen. He was so mad and went straight up to Devin, shouting, "I want you out of here! You need to find a place to live. You can't stay in this apartment. You're too fucking crazy!"

The following day I arrived at school, dropping my things on the ground because I was such a nervous wreck. As I was headed to my homeroom Sean and David came up to me. "What the hell is wrong with you? Do you know what happened to me last night?" Sean screamed.

"I didn't think he would do anything. I tried to stop him but he was so mad. I had no way of warning you. I tried to borrow a car to warn you right away," I explained tearfully.

"Do you know he has a gun? He threatened to shoot me! I should report this to the school officials. You know why I didn't? Because I feel sorry for you and your loser boyfriend."

I wished he had called the police and reported him. Maybe they would put him in jail. Sean reached out his arms to hug me. Before he did, I checked around to make sure Devin wasn't watching. I was so relieved Sean wasn't angry with me. How I wished I could tell him everything.

After school I hurried home and ran upstairs, totally forgetting Devin's threats about killing me if I ever yelled at him or told him what to do. I slammed open the bedroom door and yelled, "Why did you do this to my friends? You're evil! You're crazy! I hate you!" Devin threw me on the bed and told me take off my pants. I refused because I didn't want to get sick again. He took out his pistol and pointed at me. Crying and shaking in fear I quickly stripped off. He held my legs back and entered me hard and put my legs over his shoulders so he could go even deeper. I was trying to think of anything else and avoided making eye contact with him. When he had finished I rushed to put my jeans back on.

"I want to go home. I don't want to be with you," I told him angrily.

I felt cold metal against my mouth. "I'm going to shoot you right now." I closed my eyes. Then all of sudden Devin started to cry uncontrollably. He fell to the floor and put the shotgun down. He looked at me and said, "You're free to go home and don't come back."

"Is this for real? Can I really call my dad to come and get me?" I asked excitedly. He nodded his head. I ran into the living room where Dottie was sitting and told her I needed to use the phone. I called my dad and told him to get me. It would take him around an hour to arrive. I ran to the bedroom to pack my things and then I paced around the living room, looking out the picture window, waiting for my dad to arrive.

There was snow on the ground and it was very dull outside, like a black-and-white photo. I watched for my dad to pull up, while Devin was still in the bedroom crying. I had to get out of here before he changed his mind. Suddenly the bedroom door opened and I saw him standing in the doorway with a long silver Franchi SPAS-12 rifle.

"Tell your dad to turn around and go home. You're staying with me. If he doesn't get back in his car I'll shoot him from the window." I dissolved into tears. Dottie had gone to the store with Billy and their baby. If they had been here none of this would be happening. Billy would have thrown him down the stairs again. Devin kept looking out the window and then hiding behind the drapes.

My dad's red Cherokee Jeep finally pulled up in front of the house. I could see him sitting there looking around because he wasn't sure if he was at the right place. I ran downstairs.

"Where's your stuff?" he asked, getting out of his Jeep.

"I can't go with you. You have to go back home. I'm sorry"

"What? Please come back with me. We're going skiing with our friends. Remember Margo, your old friend? She'll be there too. She's so excited that you're coming. Forget your stuff. I'll buy you new things."

I looked up at the window. I could see the barrel of Devin's shotgun poking out from the bottom of the drapes. It was aimed right at us.

"No Dad, sorry, I've changed my mind. I'm staying here."

'Why? He's a horrible guy! Please come home. We love you and want you back."

"Please go! Please go! Don't worry about me. I'm not going with you," I yelled, pushing him back towards the driver's seat. He got in the car and drove away. I fell to the ground and let out a howl of despair as he disappeared into the distance.

Chapter 34

Devin wanted to introduce me to his childhood friend Shane. He told me Shane's parents treated him like he was their own son and were wonderful people. We arrived at a small town called Marshfield, which was practically next to Duxbury. They lived in a tiny Cape Cod-style house on a quiet street. Their front yard was messy, with toys everywhere. Devin told me Shane had three sisters and all of them had got pregnant by the age of sixteen.

Devin knocked on the front door loudly. A guy with shoulder-length hair came to the door. "Hey man! I haven't seen you in a while. Where've you been?" He grabbed Devin by the head and pretended to put him in a chokehold.

Devin grinned and said, "This is my new girlfriend Jennifer. She doesn't hear very well so you have to look at her when you speak."

Then Shane's seventeen-year-old sister Rebecca came running down the stairs and hugged Devin. She was so excited to see him. "Hey! I haven't seen you in ages! Did you see how big my son got? He's almost two now."

Devin turned to me and said, "Guess what? This girl wants to be a cop. Can you believe it?"

"Yes, it's true," she said. "I'm going to police academy when I graduate high school."

"Where are your parents?" Devin asked.

"They're both upstairs sleeping," Shane replied.

I looked at my watch. It was 1pm in the afternoon. My parents were never asleep at this time. They were hard workers and never slept late in their whole life. I was curious about these people. Who were they and how come all three of their daughters had gotten pregnant at such an early age?

Shane said, "Let's go in my room." There was a round mirror on his bedside table with coke piled in the middle. Soon they were snorting lines.

"Want a line?" Shane asked me.

"Yes, sure," I said, remembering how ecstatic and wide awake it made me feel. I got hyper-talkative almost immediately and went downstairs to see Rebecca. "Don't you like coke?" I asked her.

"No way. I'm the only one in the family that doesn't do drugs or drink."

"What about your parents?"

"Well, I don't like what they are doing. They're both addicts and sell coke and weed. You can't breathe a word of this to anyone. We used to have a good life when I was young, but Mom broke her spine in a car accident and needed something for the pain so she started on weed when I was about nine. Then Dad got involved. That's why they're both sleeping. They stay up doing drugs just about every day of the week." She looked me in the eye and said, "I don't mean to ask, but I've known Devin for years. What are you doing with him? He's not right for you. I can tell you're from a classy family."

"I'm from Duxbury."

She squealed and said, "Oh, Duxbury's a posh town. No wonder!"

I wished so badly I could tell her that Devin was forcing me to stay with him against my will. Despite all the coke, nothing would come out of my mouth. The guys thundered down the stairs and jumped on the couch to watch TV. Devin beckoned me to sit with him.

"How long are we staying here?" I asked him.

"We have to wait 'til Shane's parents wake up so I can ask them something in private." I didn't know what was going on. All I knew was Devin had taken my Social Security Income disability allowance yesterday and had a lot of cash in his wallet.

Around six o'clock, I heard footsteps coming down the stairs. Shane's parents had emerged from their room. Both of them were overweight and looked unhealthy. Shane's mom hugged Devin and said, "It's great to see you! How've you been?" Then she looked me up and down and said, "You look like a very nice girl."

Shane's father was unshaven and dressed in jeans and an old white undershirt. I was surprised to see him asking for a joint from his own son. His mom was wearing an oversized housedress. She settled down into her recliner, picked up the remote and changed the program to her favorite show. I sat across from her on the couch watching everyone take drugs.

"Hey! I need a line of coke now," Shane's mom shouted to her husband. "Please get it for me." He disappeared into the dining room and came back with a mirror with a line on it, a rolled-up dollar bill and she proceeded to snort the coke up her nose.

Then Shane said to his dad, "Devin needs to talk to you about selling weed. Can we talk about it in the kitchen?" Devin signaled to me to stay on the couch and wait. It was awkward watching Shane's mom sniffing white powder as she flipped through channels. Finally Devin came out of the dining room, smiling and holding a brown paper bag, which he shoved in his pants.

"Let's get out of here," he said to me.

I got in his car. He was really in a good mood. I said, "What did you do?"

He turned to me and said, "You and I are in the business of selling weed."

"What? I'm not selling drugs! I don't want to do it."

"You have to sell it at school."

"No way. I'm not doing it," I replied firmly.

Out of nowhere I felt a blow to my arm. I rubbed it to make the pain go away, but it hurt so bad I started crying.

"Shut up or I'll teach you a lesson you won't forget! You'll be selling joints for two dollars each. Everyone does it at your school."

"No they don't."

"Well, you go ask them."

I had watched *Chips*, the police guys on TV my whole life and knew how easy it was to get caught with drugs. My conscience was telling me this was totally wrong. When we got back to the apartment Dottie told me my mother had called and wanted me to call her back. I looked at Devin for permission. He smirked and said, "You're out of your mind. Forget it. Come with me to bedroom so I can show you something."

He dumped around fifty joints on the bed and a small pile of packs of coke, wrapped in triangles of folded-up paper. "We'll make money from this. Let's charge three dollars a joint instead of two. Give me that pocketbook of yours." I passed him my black leather bag. It had a drawstring opening at the top and a zipper down the side, which was covered by a fold of leather to create a concealed compartment. He counted out twenty joints and put them in the hidden side pocket.

The next morning I went to school with a pit in my stomach. I knew Todd had talked about smoking weed, so I approached a friend of his called Wolfe. He had slicked-back hair and wore a thick gold necklace and a black leather jacket. I signed to him behind the bus seats at the back where no one could see.

"Are you interested buying a joint?" He said yes and took some money out of his wallet. He bought four! I was excited to make my first sale. I asked him to let me know if anyone else was interested. This was a big mistake. Within the day, the entire school knew I was selling drugs.

David came up to me and asked incredulously, "Why are you doing this? I remember when you were the nicest new girl who had ever come to this school. Now look at you. You're a common drug dealer."

I felt so ashamed, but he didn't understand my situation with Devin. All day long, kids came up to me to buy joints until I was almost out. I made a lot of cash and couldn't wait to show Devin. When I got back to the apartment I found him getting ready for work. He grabbed the cash from me and counted it.

"Cool," he said, smiling. "I'll hold on to this for when we buy a house." Of course that never happened. It was just another lie.

Chapter 35

A month later I was known as the school drug dealer. Kids would come up to me from Boston School and Randolph High to get their weed. Kathy and Joseph wouldn't walk with me to school or sit with me on the bus because they were worried I'd get caught and they'd be in trouble. So I sat at the back with Wolfe and his buddies. In those days anyone who wore a jean jacket or black leather biker jacket most likely smoked and did drugs.

As I walked back to the apartment after driving back from school, I felt like someone was following me. Then I realized the same black car that had been parked across the street at school was parked on the other side of the road. I couldn't see who was in it because all the windows were blacked out. I thought it was strange but I didn't say anything to Devin.

It was Friday and Devin had that night off work. He wanted to go drinking with his friends. I dreaded it when he got drunk because he'd always pull his gun out on me while I was sleeping and tell me not to move an inch. He was in the living room with Ronnie, his girlfriend Lucy, Crazy Nick and his girlfriend Jill. They had been waiting for me to get back from school to go out partying with them.

"Did you sell any joints today?" Devin demanded.

"Of course I did," I replied, pulling out a wad of cash from my purse. All the joints were gone because everyone wanted them for the weekend. They knew I sold strong, pure weed.

"Great! We're going to the liquor store. But first I need to load you up," Devin said. He put a plastic bag solidly packed with weed into the side pocket of my handbag. "We need to get some beer from the liquor store. After that we'll go over Tony's to roll some joints for rest of the night."

I sat in the back of the car while Crazy Nick sat up front with Devin. Ronnie had his own car and followed us over there because he needed to buy beer too. We all pulled up in front of the liquor store. It was still light outside as it was only late afternoon. I stayed behind and chatted with Jill. Lucy, the loud-mouthed Italian girl came over to chat with us through the window.

All three guys were in the store when suddenly around six undercover police cars pulled up around us with their lights flashing and sirens blaring. They leapt out and surrounded the car. I was shaken to see so many undercover police officers in their black pants, black shirts and badges. One of them was even wearing a black mask to hide his face.

"What the fuck's happening?" Lucy exclaimed.

The police drew their guns and ordered us to get out of the car and put our hands on the hood. I was petrified because I had all that weed in my handbag. I was so screwed! This could mean years in jail.

The undercover sergeant in charge said to me, "Do you know why we're here?"

I said, "No." He told me that someone from school had called and ratted me out. I was in a shock and I asked who. He smiled and said the informant's name was Todd. I was so angry! I couldn't believe Todd would do this to me. What a jerk! Wait until I told his friend Wolfe. He'd be so mad because he was getting the best joints from me. Then the sergeant said he wasn't supposed to reveal his name.

Out of corner of my eye, I could see Devin and his two buddies with their bags of beer. The undercover cops had made them kneel down and put their hands behind their heads on the sidewalk. People were gathered at the street corner, watching the entertainment. The sergeant took Lucy's handbag and emptied it out onto the hood of the car. Her lipstick rolled off onto the ground.

"How dare you dump everything out!" she yelled, trying to grab her stuff. The sergeant got hold of her birth control pills, looked at them and said, "You missed two days," and laughed. Then he yelled, "You better watch yourself or I'll arrest you for tampering with evidence and disturbing the peace."

Another three police officers questioned the guys on the sidewalk. I could see Devin using hand signals and mouthing that he would take the blame if the officer found drugs in my purse. As Lucy was screaming at him, the officer tipped the contents of my pocketbook onto the hood. Out fell my make-up, my little brush and a wallet full of photos. I didn't have much. I was so nervous and I could feel my heart beating out of my chest. But I tried to act cool and cooperated with the sergeant, only speaking when I was spoken to, unlike Lucy who was ranting about her rights. He was so distracted by her that he didn't notice the hidden zipper in my purse. He was too busy yelling at Lucy, to check my bag carefully. Finally he threw it at me and told me to put everything back inside.

He grabbed Lucy, put handcuffs on her and pushed her into the back of a police car. Then he looked at me and said, "Todd better not be lying about you. Please step onto the sidewalk and sit down. Wait there and I'll tell you what to do next. I'm going to check your boyfriend's pockets and his car."

I didn't say a word. My plan was to make me his favorite so he would let me go without any more questioning. He opened all the car doors and four men searched the vehicle from top to bottom. They threw all the maps and books out of the glove compartment and yanked off the silver cross on a chain dangling from rearview mirror.

The sergeant walked over to Devin, took two beers out of his brown paper bag, opened them up, walked back to the car and poured them onto the floor of the passenger seat. They hadn't found anything and he wasn't happy.

He stared at me directly and said, "You better not deal drugs again. I'll be watching you from now on. You can go to jail for up to ten years for dealing. This is your lucky night, but I'm arresting your boyfriend for outstanding warrants. You shouldn't be with that scumbag. You can do better than that."

He was yelling at me so Devin could hear. Devin started screaming back at him, "Fuck you, man!"

He went back to Devin, turned him around, put his hands behind his back, cuffed him and arrested him right there in front of everyone. Devin wanted to speak to me but the sergeant told him sternly, "You lost that privilege. You can't speak to her or even look at her!" They hauled him away in the back of the police car. I could see him kicking in the back seat and slamming his head against the window, so they reopened the car, forced his feet up to his hands, hogtied him and threw him back on the seat lying down. I was stunned that I had got away with it. Thanks to Lucy they never found that lump of weed.

"Oh my god, you are so damn lucky you didn't get caught," Lucy said a hundred times.

All the undercover cars left and Nick and Ronnie said, "Bad timing for him to go to jail on a Friday night. He won't get out 'til next Monday, after he's seen the judge."

I didn't want to carry the weed anymore, so I told them Devin had put it in my bag and one of them had to take it from me now. "No way!" They kept saying, "Oh my god. you could have gotten arrested!"

They were hollering so loud how they couldn't believe I'd got away with it. Lucy said, "Thank goodness I made a scene otherwise you would have been caught, no question."

"Let's go back to the apartment and I'll hide it for you," Crazy Nick offered.

I drove back the apartment with the sickly smell of stale beer from the puddle on the carpet next to me. I knew the police in Duxbury would never do something like that. The downtown city police were meaner, probably because they dealt with lowlifes every day. I had no clue how to bail Devin out of jail because I'd never done it before; plus I didn't have any money. I was confused and didn't care, so I went to bed early to catch up on my sleep. Early in the morning, around 7am, I was jolted wide awake by Ronnie shaking my leg and telling me wake up.

"Hold on, so I can grab my hearing aids and put them in," I croaked, still half asleep.

"Devin called you so many times last night, saying you had to bail him out."

"But I don't have the money!"

"He's mad as hell because he has to stay in jail 'til Monday, 'til the courthouse opens. He asked for you so many times but you were asleep. He needs you to be awake when he calls from the prison phone. It's hard for him to call from there."

"Okay," I groaned and went back to sleep.

I decided to see my parents that weekend because Devin would never normally let me visit them. I showered to rid myself of the smell of cigarettes and tried to fix myself up so they wouldn't suspect anything was wrong. Then I told Ronnie I was going out and would be back later that night.

Dottie looked horrified and said, "That's not a good idea. What if he calls? He'll throw a fit when he finds out you're not here. He's only allowed to make one call a day."

"I can't hear the phone very well so it would be pointless. Please just take the call. Make excuses for me please."

Dottie said, "I'll try."

My parents were happy to see me and Dad said he'd take us all out for lunch at my favorite restaurant. Nobody said a word about

Devin, so I pretended he didn't exist. It was so comforting to see my pink bedroom was still the same except for some of my mom's craft stuff on my desk.

After we got back from the restaurant I climbed into bed and watched TV until I fell asleep, safe under my fluffy comforter. The following day I went to the beach with my parents and brother. It felt just like old times. Then my mother ruined it by mentioning Devin's name. "So when are you moving back home and leaving him for good?" she asked, as we walked along the sand.

"Please don't remind me about him. I don't want to talk about it."

"It's obvious you don't love him. You're so happy being here away from him. Just come home!"

On Sunday night I didn't want to leave. I kept looking at Devin's banged-up rust-colored car in the driveway and thought about taking off to California and disappearing. But then he'd come after my family. Or he'd track me down by finding out where my disability allowance was being sent, since he knew my social security number by heart.

I pulled up to the grim red-brick building and saw Dottie and everyone hanging out on the steps smoking cigarettes. "Do you have any idea how many times he called? He just about bit our heads off asking where you were. He's coming home tomorrow and wants you to go to the courthouse," Dottie said angrily.

"I can't do it! I have to be at school. If I miss any more days I won't graduate!"

"You'll never graduate from high school," she said. "So who cares."

"No! I'm going to school. You'll have to pick him up from the courthouse if you're such a good friend."

I went to school the next day, looking all refreshed. Some of the boys looked confused because I didn't look exhausted like usual. My heart was pounding as I watched the clock getting nearer the time I'd have to face Devin. He'd be home by now. I prayed he wasn't waiting outside the school to beat me up.

David came up to me and said, "This morning you looked so happy. Now you look like you're having a nervous breakdown. What's going on?"

"Nothing's going on. Please stop worrying about me."

"How many times do I need to tell you that you have to break up with that boyfriend of yours?"

"I'm trying," I said weakly.

Outside the apartment Devin was sitting on the steps with a look of fury on his face. I was scared to get out of the car. He barged up to my car door, opened it, put his hands around my neck, dragged me upstairs and pushed me onto the bed. "Where the fuck have you been?" he screamed, with spit flying from his mouth. "You weren't here when I called and you didn't pick me up at the courthouse. You didn't even try to get the money to bail me out of jail. You just left me to rot in there!"

He started to punch me in the face, arms and back. Then he hit me in the stomach and smashed his fist into my nose again. It was bleeding all over the place. I kept screaming for him to stop. I truly believed he was going to kill me. Then he put me in a headlock as if he was going to break my neck by twisting it. I put my hands up and made an 'I love you' sign. Slowly he let go of my head.

"I'm sorry. I didn't know how to get to the courthouse because I've never been there before and the school gave me a warning, so I had to go."

"You have to stay in bed for the rest of the night. You're only allowed to go to the kitchen or watch TV while I'm at work tonight. I'll make sure everyone knows."

There was a loud banging on the door. Billy and Crazy Nick were standing outside. "What the fuck did you do to her?" Billy shouted. I was dripping blood from my nose and one of my eyes was red.

"This is none of your fucking business! Leave us alone!"

Billy grabbed Devin by the shoulders, pushed him into the hallway and threw him towards the stairs. He went tumbling backwards. "Get your stuff out of my apartment and don't come back!" he yelled. "She can stay here 'til you find another place. Now fuck off, you piece of shit!"

Billy and Dottie went to the kitchen and got some damp paper towels to wipe the blood off me. "Jesus Jennifer," Billy said, breathless with anger. "You have to leave that shmuck and go back home to your parents. He's going to kill you one of these days. He can't come back here. We have a baby to take care of."

Billy went to the store. As he was leaving the house he saw Devin sitting on the steps with a gun pointed at his own head. Billy yanked the gun out of his hand and said, "No, you're not going to do that, you idiot." He took the gun with him to his car. If only he had let him blow his brains out.

My nose was a little swollen the next morning but I managed to hide it with lots of foundation and powder, but the students still stared at me as if something didn't look right. I saw Todd sitting at the back of the bus laughing. He couldn't look me in the eye because he'd grassed on me to the police. I had made my mind up never to sell weed or smoke it either. Devin was fine with my decision and never asked me to deal drugs again.

Chapter 36

Devin found us a place in the worst part of town, where the addicts and homeless people lived. It was in a dilapidated Victorian building with a spiral staircase going up the middle to the apartments on each floor. We didn't have to put a security deposit down because we had to clean up the mess from the last tenants. There was trash piled high everywhere. I saw a filthy diaper stuck to the wall, with roaches crawling all over it, and rotting food everywhere. I was in tears and wanted to go home. Devin got his gun out and ordered me to keep cleaning. Everywhere I looked I wanted to gag. I could hardly bring myself to touch the stinking garbage. It took me three days to get all the crap out and scrub everything down with Lysol and bleach.

We were the only white people in the building. Everyone else was black and hooked on heroin. Devin put three padlocks on the inside of the front door. Every time he went out I had to lock myself in. He'd listen for every click to make sure I'd turned the mechanism all the way. Then I'd pass him the keys under the door.

One day, we needed to go back to Marshfield to visit to one of Devin's buddies, Wyatt, who lived with his wife Debbie and their two little girls. Wyatt offered Devin a beer right away. Oh no, I thought, Devin turned even more demonic with alcohol in his system. I was nervous and smoked one cigarette after another. Debbie asked me if I was alright. I told her I was fine and sat there quietly watching as Devin poured beers down his throat. Then he started howling with laughter and rolling on the floor, drunk out of his mind.

It was after 1am in the morning and I was extremely tired. There'd been a snowstorm and I didn't want to drive on the icy roads, with Devin asleep in the passenger seat, so I asked Debbie if we could stay overnight. She told me we could sleep in the guest bedroom upstairs. Half an hour later, Devin woke me up, pulled me out of bed by my hair, threw me on the floor and demanded a blowjob. His gun was at my head.

"I'm going to shoot you right now if you don't do it properly, you bitch," he said, waving his penis in my face. Suddenly the door opened and light came in from the hallway. It was their four-year-old girl. She stared at us, transfixed in shock. Thank god we didn't have the lights on, so she didn't see anything. Devin quickly zipped up his pants and told the girl to leave.

"I heard you crying," she said, looking at me. I took her hand and led her back to her bedroom next door.

"It's okay," I reassured her. "I was just crying because I miss my home."

She looked at me all wide-eyed and said, "That man looks like a monster. Why did he have a gun in his hand? I saw him pointing it at your head. Why did he do that?" I told her everything was okay and she had to go to bed. It was so hard for me to return to the bedroom. He was waiting for me in the twin bed, with his pistol directed straight at me.

"Sleep on the edge of the bed," he commanded. "If I feel you shift and inch I'll pull the trigger." When he was asleep I looked around for the car keys but I couldn't find them. About an hour later Devin woke up and told me we were leaving. He wanted me to drive us back to Boston.

"But I can't see in this weather! Look at the snow! The roads are dangerous!"

Outside, he dragged me to the passenger side and said, "Okay, get in. I'm driving." He drove like a lunatic, far too fast for the icy roads.

"Oh my god!" I screamed in horror. "We're going to crash!"

Not far from the house he lost control and we slammed into a ditch full of snow by the side of the road. I was sure the car would blow up, so I squeezed myself out of the window and fell onto the freezing ground. Further up the road I saw the lights inside a Chinese restaurant. I left Devin slumped over in the driver's seat and ran into the foyer, crying hysterically. The Chinese cooks stared at me as I tried to put a dime into the payphone on the wall to call 911, but I couldn't hear anything at the other end. I cried to one of the workers to help me. One of them took the receiver and explained to the operator that there was an emergency and gave them the address of the restaurant.

Devin burst in through the door and ran towards me, limping, and punched me in the face, knocking me to the ground. "Don't call the police you fool! You know I have a warrant on me!"

The Chinese man shouted at him to leave me alone. Devin put his fist up the air and started to lunge towards him. At that moment some police officers, who were at the scene of the accident, ran in and arrested Devin for assaulting me and for threatening behavior. They handcuffed him and marched him to the other side of restaurant. They had been outside for some time because someone else had already called them.

I was still crying and hurt from being punched on the side of my head. An ambulance arrived and the paramedics wanted to take me to hospital. I said no, because I wasn't seriously injured, and signed a waiver to say I had refused medical attention. I gave the police Shane's number and they asked him to come and get me.

Devin was raging mad that he'd been arrested again. The next morning he got out of jail and immediately came after me. He wrenched me out of bed while I was asleep, jolting me wide awake in terror.

"Please, please let go of me! Let me go home to my family. I promise I won't tell anyone about you and your threats," I begged.

"Oh no," he snarled. "You're staying with me."

Chapter 37

Devin wanted to make money selling cocaine, so he drove us back to Marshfield to meet one of Shane's mafia connections, a drug dealer who lived in a huge house in a wealthy neighborhood.

"Do exactly what I tell you to do. Say nothing and pretend you can't hear or speak. These are dangerous people. They'll kill you if you put a foot wrong."

Two tall men wearing sunglasses, dressed in sharp suits, with gun holsters, stood guard outside of the front door. It was like a scene from *The Godfather*. One of them opened his jacket to show us he had a gun. Devin handed him a piece of paper with a code word written on it that Billy had given him. They let us in and told us to go into the kitchen. I was astounded at what I saw. The mafia boss was sitting behind a round table with a set of scales next to a huge pile of lumpy white powder and stacks of bags filled with cocaine. He looked like a regular guy, except he had a gun holster under his armpit.

He pointed at me immediately and said, "Who's that? I don't allow any bitches in here. They have big mouths."

Devin looked at him and laughed. "Don't worry, she's deaf. She can't speak either."

The mafia boss seemed to relax, then picked up a razor blade and chopped up a line on a small oblong mirror for Devin to sample. As Devin was sniffing the coke, the mafia boss came up to me and looked me up and down.

"Wow, she's pretty!" he said. "How about I trade her for sex and give you some extra coke?"

Devin got annoyed. "No, she's mine. No one touches her but me."

A bodyguard took a pistol from inside his jacket. His boss smiled and waved his hand at him, saying, "No, no, it's okay." But he refused to give up, and after a couple of minutes he said, "How about I give you half an ounce free if you let me have sex with her?"

"It's a deal," Devin responded, quick as a flash.

I looked at him in horror and said, "Please don't do this!"

"What the fuck! I thought you said she couldn't hear or talk!" The mafia boss got angry and glared at Devin. Then he grabbed me by my hair and pulled me towards to him. "Let's go," he said, nudging me to walk in front of him, with a gun pressed into my back. I went up the long curved black-and-white marble steps to his bedroom. It was decorated in black and red and had a king-sized bed, with mirrors above it on the ceiling.

He shut the door and I began to cry. "Take your clothes off and stand at the end of the bed and bend over," he ordered. "Don't worry, dear. I'll be gentle with you." I stripped naked, stood as instructed and tried to breathe, despite being rigid with fear and trembling from head to toe. He entered me from behind. His penis was larger than Devin's and there was a sharp pain inside every time he banged away at me. After he had climaxed, he pulled out and slapped me across my backside.

"That was good. Now get dressed. We're going back downstairs." He gripped my arm tightly as we made our way down to the kitchen, then he shoved me back over to Devin. "Come over here and have some of this," he said to me. "I have to test you and make sure you're not a cop. Then he said to Devin, "So what is it that you want from me?"

"So, the word is you're the best supplier around. I can make a lot of money for you if you give me a cut of all the deals I make."

"Well, since you know Billy and his family I'll trust you. There's just one thing. If you don't give me the money you get from selling this stuff, my guys will come after you and your girlfriend and cut your legs off." I jumped in fright when he said that. Then he shoved a huge block of cocaine the size of a brick into a brown paper bag. "You have one month to turn this into cash. I'll give you more if you don't screw me over. I want two hundred bucks a gram, minimum one fifty."

"Don't worry, you'll get all your money back," Devin replied. He casually picked up the bag like it was a take-out from McDonald's and we walked back to the car, with the bodyguards following closely behind. Devin was howling with excitement at all the money he was going to make, saying he could buy a house and a new car. It was all garbage talk. The idiot was addicted to cocaine and would probably snort the lot. I wondered what they would use to chop our legs off: an axe, a saw or an electric turkey knife? Would I die or end up in a wheelchair?

Chapter 38

Back at our apartment, Devin was in the living room snorting lines of cocaine from a mirror. "Here, have some," he said to me. I sniffed up a few lines and whoosh! I felt like I was on top of the world. I had so much energy I could run up the Empire State Building and back. We were watching TV and kept refueling every hour.

Later that night, Devin started acting all strange, saying, "Hey, did you see that? That mouse is crawling all over place. Look at it!" He was standing on the couch and following this imaginary creature with his finger.

"There's nothing there," I told him, noticing his eyes were very wide and bloodshot. I kept telling him there was nothing there and he was imagining things. This was another weird side of him I hadn't seen before.

The next day was Thanksgiving. I told Devin I had to go home or my parents would think he was holding me against my will. I pleaded with him to let me go and promised to return.

"You're not taking the car. I'll drop you off and pick you up. Don't worry. I don't want to join your family. They don't like me and the feeling's mutual."

"Okay. What time will you pick me up?"

"I'll be there at eight o'clock in the evening, sharp."

I was so excited to see my family and my cousins Kristen and Jamie. My Aunt Ann and Uncle Jimmy were there, as well my grandparents and my other grandma. Everyone was happy to see me but they were baffled and shocked by my ghostly appearance. I'd lost so much weight from snorting cocaine and forgetting to eat. I was as skinny as a toothpick.

"What happened to you?" Kristen said with tears in her eyes. "You don't look like the Jennifer I know. Please stop whatever you're doing to yourself."

My grandparents were yelling in Italian back and forth. I knew they were arguing about me because of the way they were assessing me up and down.

"Why do you have to live with that useless shrimp?" Grandpa Bruno said, waving his hands in the air. "You need to come home now!"

I felt a pang of sadness. I wished desperately that I could find a way out of this. My godfather Tom worked as a secret agent and had protected President Ronald Reagan several times. He came up to me in the hallway and said, "I know you're doing cocaine. I could tell right away. You need to come back to your family right now." I ignored all of their demands for the sake of keeping them alive.

I had a great time eating Thanksgiving dinner with them. All of the delicious food had been made by my mother and Grammy Bruno. Later that evening, everyone had gone home except Tom. It was 8:30pm and Devin still hadn't shown up. I called him but there was no answer.

Tom said, "I can drive you over there and drop you off."

"Sure," I said and got into his brand-new BMW. As he was driving he kept glancing over at me.

"Do you need me to help get you out of your situation?" I could see he had a gun in his holster under his arm. I didn't want him to get killed, knowing how unpredictable Devin was.

"No, I'm fine, really," I told him.

The entire journey to the apartment he repeated that he could help me. All I had to do was get my stuff and he'd take me back home. "This is a dangerous neighborhood. I'm not happy you're living here," he said, when we arrived at the apartment.

"It's okay. I'll go inside alone. Thanks so much for the ride."

Tom wrote his home phone number on the back of his business card. "If you need my help, call me. I'll come and get you out of here."

When I opened the front door, Devin was on the staircase, laughing and throwing water at several black guys who were trying to get away from him. There were about seven floors in the building, with stairs that circled to the top, so there was a clear view of the apartments on each floor. Most of the doors were open and people were throwing food and water at each other. I was thankful that Tom hadn't seen this because he would have called the police for sure. As soon as they saw me everyone went silent. Then one of the black guys whistled and said, "Hey baby, do you want to hook up with me?"

Devin went berserk and ran up the stairs shouting, "I'm going to get my machine gun and kill you!"

One of the guys, who knew he had guns, grabbed his legs. The black guy yelled back, "Come on, bring it on! Shoot me, fool!"

It took six men to hold Devin down and stop him from getting his guns. I ran past him up the stairs to our apartment and threw his machine gun under the bed. It took an hour for him to calm down. After all the drama was over, he wanted me to snort cocaine with him. I had more than usual and soon I could feel my heart beating way too fast. I couldn't breathe!

"Help, I'm dying! I can't breathe!" I told Devin in a panic. "You need to call 911."

"Hell no, I'm not getting us both in trouble."

I ran into the bathroom to look at myself. The pupils of my eyes were enlarged. I prayed to God to not let me die and promised Him I wouldn't touch cocaine ever again. I forced myself to stay awake so I didn't pass away in my sleep and I kept drinking lots of water. About six hours later, I was shaking, feeling cold and sick, and started to vomit.

I couldn't move for three days. I was so ill from withdrawal and quitting cold turkey. I felt so much better, getting back to my healthy old self and went to bed early for the first time in ages. Without the cocaine in my system I didn't lie awake anymore. Meanwhile Devin was going at it harder than ever. Weeks had passed and Devin still hadn't sold any of the brick of cocaine. I kept nagging him to stop using it all for himself.

"Shut up and mind your own business. I know what I'm doing," he kept telling me.

I dreaded the day the mafia boss came after him for his money. Surges of sickening fear would take over my body every day. I thought things couldn't get much worse. But then an even uglier chapter added itself to the horror story of my life.

Chapter 39

I heard a knock on the door. Devin was sitting on the couch watching TV. He told me to answer it. A little girl, about nine years old, was standing outside holding a cage with a beautiful, gray-haired rabbit inside.

"Please can you look after my bunny? My dad told me I have to get rid of it," she said tearfully. "Her name is Carrots. I have everything for her cage and she's free."

With Devin's permission I took the rabbit, telling her she could stop by when Devin was home to visit the pet. She showed me how to put the water bottle between the cage bars and how to line the bottom with newspaper. It was great having another living creature to keep me company while Devin was out drinking. I left her cage open and let her run around the spare room. I even taught her to come to me when I called her name and she'd hop up onto my lap.

One day Devin came home drunk and loaded with cocaine. He sat next to me on the couch to watch TV. Carrots came bounding out of her room and jumped on my lap as usual.

"Hey, it's not fair that she doesn't come to me. Hey, Carrots, come here! Sit on my lap!" Devin ordered. The rabbit refused to go over to him because I truly believed she could sense danger.

"Carrots is with me all the time. She's my baby," I told him. "She's never spent any time with you. She needs to get to know you first. I'll put her back in her cage." Devin slapped my face and pulled the rabbit out of my hands.

"No!" I yelled, "No!" I tried to save her but everything happened too fast. He held her by the ears and ran into the spare bedroom and locked the door. I begged him not to hurt Carrots and turned my hearing aids up so I could tell what was happening. I could feel vibrations as Devin slammed the rabbit against the wall.

"Please don't do that to her," I screamed. "Please!"

Fifteen minutes later, he came out with the rabbit's body hanging down limply from his fist. Her face was all bloody and bashed in. I couldn't look because I was scared that I would be next. He dropped it in a plastic trash bag and went outside to throw it in the dumpster. My heart was crushed. I couldn't stop crying. That poor creature was innocent and hadn't done anything wrong. I could never forgive him for this. The little girl came back a week later to check on her bunny and it broke my heart to lie and say she had got sick and died. She ran off crying.

Today I still remember everything so clearly and it bothers me so much. Every time I go to country fairs or farms and I see a gray bunny there's a pain in my heart. It's a memory I hate to relive.

A few weeks later, got called into the principal's office. My parents and several school officials were there too. The principal handed me a paper. It said I couldn't graduate with my class. I started to cry and begged them not to do this. They looked at me and said, "You've missed too many school days and have been late for class too many times. You need to make up your missing school work. We'll give you your diploma here in this office after you've caught up."

Another classmate, Cathy, had the same issue as me, which made me feel a little better. She went to see our classmates graduate and get their diplomas on the stage. I refused to go because I couldn't bear to see everyone in their gowns and caps. It was a very sad day for me. I made up the classes and got my diploma but I always felt I had missed out on one of the most important days of my life. My classmates and I parted ways and I didn't see most of them for years.

They were all looking forward to going to college, while I was looking at living on the streets. We had run out of money and couldn't afford to pay the rent on the apartment. Devin was spending all of the money on alcohol and cocaine. The block from the dealer had long since disappeared.

Devin said I could move back home on one condition, that he was allowed to live there too. My parents reluctantly agreed to let him stay in the spare room until he found a place to live. We got our stuff, loaded up the car and drove to Duxbury. I was so nervous because I didn't want my parents to see what a mess Devin was with his alcohol and drugs.

One night, Devin came home at two o'clock in the morning. Dad woke me up and told me he was in the hallway, talking nonsense and drunk. I was sick to my stomach and scared he'd shoot everyone. I told him he had to leave and go to his friend's house, but he refused to go, so my dad called the police. They arrested him because of a previous warrant and took him off to spend the night in jail. My dad packed up all his belongings and put them in the garage. The smell of his booze still lingered in the air in the hallway.

"That crazy guy isn't welcome here. Tell him he's out." I was so ashamed I'd brought this disgusting person into my parents' home and was so frustrated that I couldn't tell them why.

Devin received a court order to go to rehab for a few days and then to attend a halfway house four towns away from where we lived. He demanded that I visited him every day. I had to drive all the way over there in his unreliable heap. My parents had given my old Monte Carlo to my brother and were worried that I'd break down in a dangerous area, so they put down a deposit on a car for me, provided I made the monthly payments. I loved my new white Chevrolet Corsica.

I drove to see Devin for the first time. His rehab facility was a huge five-story Victorian house. The ground floor was surrounded by a screened-in deck, with rocking chairs. On the outside of the building, a metal stairway zigzagged all the way up to the top floor. I parked my car in a dirt parking lot. Judging by the vehicles in here the residents of this place were not among life's success stories. My gleaming new Chevy looked out of place next to the old pick-up truck with a camper on the top and all the other rust buckets.

Devin got up quickly when he saw me and told me I looked great. Then he said he'd got us two ATVs, one dark blue and one bright yellow, from a guy who owed him money for drugs. He demonstrated how to operate the vehicle in the front yard. There were no complicated stick shifts and everything was automatic.

"Let's go offsite and ride our ATVs in the woods and smoke a joint," he said, winking at me.

"I can't invite you to my room because it's a men only house. No women are allowed in except Betty, the lady pig supervisor. I live right up there in the attic," he said, pointing to the top of the house. "You're going to climb up the fire escape to my room after we've ridden our ATVs."

I looked at the side of the house and realized it was about a sixty-five-foot climb to get to the top. "No way. I can't get up those stairs. They look like they'll collapse."

He gave me the dead eye and said, "Do it or I'll kill you when I get out of here."

I got on my yellow ATV and raced around the house and into the woods, following Devin. I enjoyed riding in the wind. I was laughing so hard that people came outside to see what was going on. When it was getting dark we parked our vehicles at the back of the house and chained them up.

"Now go up the stairs," Devin instructed. "I'll go into the house to distract the pig and everyone else from looking out of the window. Give me a couple of minutes."

I was very nervous about going up the open metal treads. I slowly put my feet on each step, praying it would hold. I passed the first window and saw four guys watching TV with Devin talking to them to distract them. The rest of the windows on the floors above were blocked by white blinds. I reached the fifth floor and Devin opened the window and pulled me inside. I was shaking because I'd never climbed that high in my life.

His room was very small. There was just a twin-sized bed, a wooden nightstand table and a bureau with a mirror above it. The floors and ceiling were covered in cedar wood paneling. Devin ordered me to take my clothes off and get on the bed.

"I bought a Polaroid camera so I can take pictures of you naked. It has an automatic ten-second timer so I can be in the picture with you, having sex." He ordered me to get into various positions. Then he told me to lie on my back so he could get a close-up of my vagina. Photos were spewing out of his camera. He got a bar stool and set the camera on it, took his clothes off and pressed the timer. He kept fucking me and rushing back to the camera until all the film had run out. Then he laid all the wet Polaroid photos across his table. (The worst part of this story is that eventually my dad saw all these pornographic images when he went to clear out our apartment a couple of years later. That thought still mortifies me.)

I put my clothes on and Devin went downstairs to make sure Betty wasn't going to check on him. Finally, he told me it was clear for me to go back down the fire exit. It was dark and there were moths flying around the lights at the windows. When I reached the ground I hurried to my car and drove home.

Every day for the next two months I repeated this drill and Timothy, the old man always got up from his chair to greet me and shook my hand every time I arrived. Then one day I saw an ambulance and police parked at the house. Devin was standing outside along with several men who were watching the paramedics carry a body bag out on a stretcher.

"Timothy died," Devin told me, "Betty found him on the floor in his bedroom with his arms sticking straight up and legs all stiff and straight and his eyes were wide open. He had a heart attack in middle of the night."

I felt sad and sorry for Timothy because he had always smiled and greeted when I came over.

"Can we go to his funeral?" I asked. I was surprised when Devin said, "Yes. I'll find out when it is."

His burial was scheduled three days later. I got dressed in black and picked Devin up along with a friend of his and drove to the funeral home. I was expecting maybe a hundred people to show up but we were the only people there.

I saw an open casket and rows of empty chairs. There was a basket of flowers on each side of his coffin. I looked inside the coffin to make sure we were at the right funeral. Why was no one else here? I asked the funeral director if we were early. He looked at me and said, "You are on time. His sister will be arriving very soon from out of state."

I took my seat in the third row. Maybe Betty from the halfway house would show up? I looked around expecting a crowd to walk in at any moment but no one came.

Finally an old lady in a brown fur coat and hat arrived with two young girls holding onto her arms. She walked up to the coffin, glared at the body for a moment and then sat down in the front row. I just didn't get it. She quickly said something to the funeral director. Devin looked at me and said, "They aren't going to do any readings. They want to take his body now to the cemetery and get this over with."

We got into the hearse and followed them out to the cemetery. Devin laughed saying, "This is the quickest funeral in history! He must have pissed a lot of people off 'cos nobody showed up!"

I was confused because Timothy was always so friendly to me. I didn't understand it.

As we arrived the coffin was being carried to its excavated resting place. The old lady and her two attendees stood by her side and watched. There wasn't even a priest to say the last rights.

The lady watched them lower the coffin in the grave before going over and spitting on the coffin. The she turned around and walked away. I rushed up to her. She stopped and looked at me coldly. "I'm truly sorry for your loss," I said.

"He is a no good brother to me. Everyone in the family hated him," she replied.

"If you don't mind me asking, why was that? He was always very friendly to me."

She pointed her finger at me and said, "Well he wasn't like that when he was drinking. He was a mean son of a bitch. He ruined my life and everyone else's. He sexually molested me when I was little and did the same thing to his daughters and his granddaughters."

I was stunned into silence.

"I had to come and spit on his coffin to make myself feel better," she added. She turned around and walked away with her two granddaughters smiling at me as they left. At that moment I realized I wanted the church at my funeral to be packed with people who thought fondly of me. I vowed to always treat everyone with kindness so I would not leave this earth alone.

Chapter 41

Devin left the halfway house and moved in with his boss's secretary Elaine. She had a younger boyfriend called Randy who worked at the same garage as Devin, fixing up RV camping trailers. Devin never lasted long at any of his jobs or living arrangements. He was always moving because he owed the mafia guy more than twenty-five thousand dollars for the cocaine.

Elaine was divorced, had two grown sons and wanted the extra income from renting one of the bedrooms in her big colonial-style house, which was about ten minutes away from where I lived with my parents.

One day I stopped by the house. A friend of Devin's came running out onto the lawn just as I was pulling up into the driveway. He must have seen me coming. Devin chased after him, threw him on the ground and put his hand over his mouth to stop him talking to me. I later found out that he was going to tell me Devin was seeing someone else.

I joined Devin to watch a football game with Elaine's churchgoer friends. I sat on the couch next to her son's girlfriend, while Devin lay on his belly on the floor. An hour later Randy noticed that Devin's face was on the floor. He tapped him on the shoulder and tried to wake him up. "He's a faker and just wants attention. There's nothing wrong with him," Randy said, shaking him and rolling him over. After five minutes with no response Elaine called 911. An ambulance and fire truck arrived. The first responders worked on him but he was still unconscious, so they took him away on a stretcher. I told Elaine I'd meet them at the hospital later. But, as always, I went home.

My mom knocked on my bedroom door and said Elaine and Randy wanted to know where I was. Reluctantly I drove to see Devin. A doctor explained that he had had a seizure that had knocked him out cold, but he was awake now. He took us to his room, where he was sitting up in bed smiling. I didn't want to be near him or look at him so I quietly stood next to his bed.

"Are you disappointed I didn't die?" he smirked. "Well it's too bad. You're stuck with me."

About a week later, I rushed to meet Devin at Elaine's house. I had to be there at four o'clock and was running late. The front door was open, which was unusual. I went inside, calling out to see if anyone was home and saw Devin sitting in a chair holding a shotgun to his head.

"I'm going to kill myself right now."

"Please don't do that," I said, trying to appear concerned. In an instant he grabbed my arm and pulled me towards him.

"Get down on the floor! Kneel!" he ordered. "Now open your mouth!" He turned the shotgun around and screamed, "Do it!" I opened my mouth and he shoved the shotgun into it. I signed 'I love you' in the air like always. "I'm going to kill you and then shoot myself."

After a few moments he took the gun out of my mouth, put it down and started to cry. I ran to the kitchen and called the police, saying, "Please come now! It's an emergency. He has guns and he tried to kill me!"

Ten minutes later, five police cars pulled up in a zigzag formation on the front lawn. I had called my brother Antonio to come over too because I was so frightened. Devin ran into the kitchen and kicked me hard on my leg and commanded, "Get down on the floor! I'm going to kill your brother when he gets here."

Through the picture window I could see the police were using a megaphone to ask Devin to come out with his hands above his head.

"You'd better not tell them what I did to you. When I get out of jail I swear to god I'll kill you and your family, including that nasty old grandfather of yours."

Eventually, after about half an hour, he gave up. He put his hands up behind his head and went outside, where he was arrested on the spot. They put his shotgun in the trunk and pushed him into the back of a police car. My brother came running up and asked what was going on. The police told him they were dealing with a suicide attempt and were taking Devin to a psychiatric hospital for evaluation.

"What?" I said. "Why aren't you arresting him for threatening to kill me?"

I didn't leave my bedroom for days. I was petrified Devin would be waiting outside to blow my brains out. But after a few days I realized he would have been put back on the strong tranquilizers they always gave him. So I began to relax and enjoy my freedom and went back to McDonalds to work part-time for a couple of weeks.

Devin was released and went back to Elaine's house. She and her sons had no idea why he'd been taken to hospital. He asked me to come and see him, reminding me that he still had his guns and a very good reason to come after me. Just like that I was thrown back into my old, unbearable life.

Chapter 42

Elaine invited me to go to an Amy Grant concert with her and her Christian friends. Devin agreed to let me go on the understanding that I was back by 5pm. He made me wear a watch so there were no excuses for being late. The concert started at 1pm but we left at 10am to make sure we were near the front of the stage with our lawn chairs and blankets.

The concert didn't actually start until 3pm. My nerves were on edge, realizing I would never make it back in time. I started to shake and felt sick. I had to go to the bathroom because I thought I was going to throw up. It was nearly 8pm. I just wanted to die right there. I kept asking Elaine when we were going to leave and she kept saying, "Soon."

We finally left around 9pm and didn't get home until around 11pm because the parking lot was so congested. I was shaking so badly and Elaine and the others kept asking me if I was alright. Devin was standing in the driveway with the garage lights on waiting for me to arrive. Elaine's sons came out to greet us. Everyone was telling them how wonderful the concert was and how much fun they had.

"Come here Jennifer," Devin said loudly. "You have to go home. Your parents are waiting for you." I felt my heart racing. I could smell alcohol on his breath. He pinched my arm and told me to get in the car. Then he pulled over into a private road and whacked me across my face, screaming, "Where the hell were you!"

I tried to explain that the concert didn't start until late and it carried on all night, with people dancing and that we couldn't get out of the parking lot.

"You were supposed to be back here at five sharp!" he bellowed, hitting the steering wheel. He looked at me and said, "I guess it's your fault that I was in a bad mood and decided to kill someone tonight."

"You did what?" I gasped.

He took a small black velvet box from the back seat, reached into it and threw pieces of something at me. Whatever they were felt heavy and wet as they landed on my lap and chest. I put the overhead lights on and looked down, staring in horror. There were bloody chopped fingers all over me and streaks of blood on my blouse.

"Oh my god!" I screamed and opened the car door to jump out.

"Stay there and don't move," he said, holding his gun at me. Then he got out of the car and threw out the rest of the fingers into the woods.

"You killed someone tonight because of me?" I shrieked in disbelief.

"Yes, look on the back seat and look on the floor."

I visualized a dead body slumped in the back seat but there was just an open wallet with a photo ID. I wanted to see who he had killed but he wouldn't let me touch the wallet. To this day I have no idea what happened to that guy. Was he murdered or did Devin just chop his fingers off as a warning? I didn't sleep all night. It took many weeks to get the image of those bloody dismembered fingers out of my head.

Chapter 43

Devin picked me up from home. He wouldn't come inside because he knew my father hated him. "I can't wait to talk to you," he said to me, suspiciously nicely. He turned into a secluded parking lot behind a doctor's office next door to a bowling alley. Nobody could see us because it was surrounded by pine trees. It was dark and very cold outside with the wet remains of snow on the ground.

I knew he'd been drinking because I could smell the beer on his breath. He had told me many times that he was sorry for his behavior when he got drunk and promised to quit. He gave me a little speech about how he wanted to be with me forever until we both died of old age. Then, to my surprise, he took out a small velvet box and held it near my face.

"Please will you marry me? I want us to be married."

I looked at him aghast and immediately said, "No."

"You bitch!" he bellowed, punching the steering wheel with his fists. I truly thought he would break his hands. I put my right hand on the door handle and slowly lifted it up, planning to run out as fast as I could. The handle made a click.

He took his .45 pistol out of his belt, grabbed my legs and landed on top of me, forcing the door to open halfway. He put his finger on the trigger and pointed it at my face, shouting, "Jennifer, you're marrying me whether you like it or not." My head was sticking halfway outside and my neck wasn't resting on anything. I kept telling him to get off me. He started to spin the cylinder as if he was playing Russian roulette. I had to do something or I'd be dead.

"You're not supposed to say no! You're supposed to say yes!" he yelled. He called out "Jennifer" three times like my name was poison. I kicked him in the groin with my heel. The gun went off with a loud bang and I could see smoke above my head. While he was bent over in pain I ran towards the bowling alley. I glanced behind and saw him limping after me. A car came towards me and I ran towards its headlights.

"Help me please!" I screamed hysterically. "I need to call the police. I'm being shot at by that guy who's chasing me!" I banged on the hood of his car out of desperation. The driver waved his hand and told me to get in fast. I saw Devin running after us and put my foot over his on the gas pedal, yelling, "Quick, he's got a gun!"

The poor guy was shaking all over. He wore glasses and was the nerdy type who didn't know how to fight or take action. I told him to calm down and take me to the police station as fast as he could. Devin had got back into his car and was chasing us like in the movies, speeding up behind us and flashing his headlights. He drove right up next to our car and yelled at us to pull over. I kept telling the driver, "No! Keep going!"

"I'll smash your car if you don't stop now!" Devin screamed.

The nerd looked at me and said, "I don't want my car to be wrecked. I just bought it." Devin swerved around to the front of the car and started to approach us on foot.

"Quick!" I told the nerd, "Run him over before he punches you out!" The nerd just sat there paralyzed with fright. I slammed my foot on the gas pedal and hit Devin in the leg. He went flying into the side of a snow bank. The nerd took my hands off the steering wheel and put his car back into park.

"No! Please put it in drive. We need to go to the police station now!"

Devin got back up with an even worse limp and started banging on the window on the driver's side. "Don't open your door! He'll kill you!" I screamed. But the nerd rolled down his window and Devin punched him in the face over and over again.

"Stop!" I shrieked in horror. "I'll go with you if you leave him alone." I told the nerd how sorry I was to trouble him. He was bleeding from his nose and mouth.

Devin hit me in the head and yelled sarcastically, "Don't you ever run away from me again. Can't you see how dangerous it is to get into a stranger's car?" He was dragging his foot along the ground and cursing at me. He blamed the nerd for driving into him, thank god, or I would surely have been beaten to death and dumped in the woods. He drove away to hide before the police arrived.

When he was sure nobody was around he parked up and said, chillingly, "Jennifer … Jennifer … Jennifer … So are you going to marry me?"

"Yes," I said quietly.

"You better tell your parents to agree to it and to pay for the wedding. You can warn them if they don't they'll never see you again. We'll move far away out of state and they'll never be able to find you." I sobbed all the way home.

The following day I told my parents I was engaged. They were both devastated and kept reminding me I was marrying an alcoholic and a loser.

"A small simple wedding is fine," I said. "It doesn't have to be expensive."

"Well, you're my daughter and I know it has been your lifetime dream to get married, but not to him. He's the wrong guy for you. You deserve so much better," my mom sighed. My dad couldn't handle the stress and walked out of the house to go somewhere alone. It was such a sad sight. Now more than ever, I couldn't tell them what was really going on.

Chapter 44

I had to try on wedding dresses at the bridal shop. My mother didn't want to go but she showed up anyway, along with Devin's foster mother. I didn't want her to spend much on this fiasco so I found a cowgirl-style dress with a matching cowgirl hat for less than $300. My mother burst into tears when she saw me in the quirky outfit. I knew it wasn't because she was happy for me. How different things would have been if I had gone to Gallaudet University and married Matt. That thought broke my heart into a million pieces. I couldn't wait to get out of there to smoke a cigarette.

I moved out of my parents' house for the third time to live in the guest suite of a ranch house owned by Devin's new boss, a single mother called Mary, who had an eight-year-old son. She owned of a construction company and had hired Devin after he was fired from his RV job for constantly having seizures and passing out.

Devin attached two padlocks to the bedroom door so he could lock me up whenever he wanted. I would hang around at the apartment watching TV, reading books and smoking. Seeing I was bored and lonely, he brought home a fluffy black chow puppy a co-worker had given him in exchange for cocaine. It was love at first sight. She was beautiful, with dark-blue eyes and perfect in every way.

"This is your puppy and I'm going to name her Coco," he announced.

I picked her up and cuddled her, saying, "Don't worry, I'll protect you no matter what."

About four days before the wedding, we went to Billy's house to hang out with his friends who were all drinking and partying. There were people jammed in every room. I didn't see where Devin went so I sat alone on the couch. A few hours later one of his friends said, "Hey, we've been looking all over for you. Your fiancé is passed out drunk. You need to take him home." They carried him to my car and put him in the passenger seat. I wanted so badly to dump him somewhere but I kept thinking about God watching me.

It was around 2am and the highway was quiet. It was pitch black because there were no street lamps for several miles. Suddenly Devin woke up and said, "Hey, where are we?" I told him we were heading home. Then I was blinded by some high-beam headlights in my rearview mirror.

I grabbed the steering wheel with both hands and kept my arms stiff to stop myself from going through the windshield because the car was coming up fast behind us. Devin grabbed his head rest as the car behind smashed into the back of us with a powerful force, propelling us up the road. I screamed because I couldn't stop. The brakes wouldn't work. We were going more than 125mph and I could feel the car wobbling and there was nothing I could do to slow it down.

Devin took the steering wheel and turned it sharply to the right. The car lifted up and rolled three times before hitting the guardrail, where it came to rest with smoke coming from the hood. My neck and legs were in terrible pain. The black car that hit us was smashed up at the front and only made it a few yards along the breakdown lane. Devin jumped out and ran to the driver's side of the car and started smacking the driver in the head. I got out of the car and collapsed on the road. The lights were on inside the black car. There was something about the driver's face that looked familiar. Someone came over to help me, while another bystander went over to restrain Devin.

Three police cars and an ambulance arrived. One of the police officers was my neighbor. He knelt down next to me and asked, "Hey, are you alright?" I told him I had pain in my legs and neck, then I started to cry. He told me to lie back down and not to move until the paramedics got there.

"That guy in that black car was drunk. He'll be getting a DUI for sure," he explained to me. "They can smell alcohol on him." Then I saw a police car taking the driver away from the scene. I didn't understand why they didn't make him do a sobriety test first.

"Why are they taking him away so quickly?" I asked my police officer neighbor. He said he didn't know and went to find out what was going on. Devin came over and walked with me as the paramedics wheeled me on a stretcher into the back of an ambulance. He looked over at me and smiled.

"Our problems are over now. We are going to sue that asshole for sure."

We got to the hospital emergency room and, after I'd been X-rayed, two men in dark suits came into the room and said something to Devin, then they all went outside to talk. About twenty minutes later Devin came back, grinning and holding some papers.

"Sign this now."

"Why? What am I signing?"

"It's an agreement. They'll give us a check if we keep quiet about this."

"Why do we have to be quiet about it?"

Devin looked at me angrily and said, "Just sign it." He disappeared with the paperwork and returned a few minutes later with a folded check in his hands. "We're rich!" he laughed. "I'll use this to buy drugs and sell them." The check was for ten thousand dollars.

"Sign the back and I can cash it," he instructed.

"Why did they give us a check?"

Hardly able to contain himself, he said, "That guy is from the famous Kennedy family. His name is John F. Kennedy Junior."

"Oh my god, really?" I gasped. I had thought he looked familiar.

"I'm going to cash this now before they change their minds. Remember, the agreement is you can't tell a soul about this, including your parents, or they'll go after us for breach of contract."

The subject was never mentioned again. Occasionally I saw John F. Kennedy Junior on the news and I felt so bad when he was killed. It made me wonder whether he was drinking that night when the plane he was piloting crashed into the ocean.

Maybe I should have said something so he would have gotten into trouble and might have gone to rehab. They probably covered up what really happened with the plane incident like they did with his car accident, to make sure his reputation was perfect in life and in death. I remember him standing there at his father's funeral when he was just a little boy and I felt so sorry for him. Maybe that's why I couldn't bring myself to harm his public image either.

My parents arrived and my mother immediately said, "This is a sign from God. Maybe He doesn't want you to get married."

The doctor said I had sprained my knees and had severe whiplash and just needed to rest for a few days. My parents took me home and I retreated to the safety of my familiar pink bedroom.

Chapter 45

The day before the wedding, my mother kept telling me I could still call it off. I told her I had to go ahead with it, but I wouldn't be able to dance or stand up for pictures because my neck hurt too much. It was just an excuse. I didn't want anyone to see how short Devin was next to me.

The doorbell rang. It was Devin, demanding to talk to me in private. I went outside to his car. "Don't take off or cancel the wedding or I'll kill everyone in the church. I mean it. Be there tomorrow."

I was in tears. I didn't want to get married to him but I had to pretend to be happy. I got out of the car and ran upstairs to my bedroom and sat on my bed trying to figure out what to do. My car was parked on the street outside my window and my suitcase was packed for the honeymoon. I could drive to California when everyone was sleeping. I got my car keys and was ready to escape when, all of sudden, I visualized all those dead bodies lying on the pews and I couldn't do it.

The next day, as he was about to walk me down the aisle, my father said, "Are you sure you want to get married? You can always back out now and leave." I told him the wedding was going ahead and we linked arms. When we got to the altar I had to stand next to Devin. I knew people were staring at us and seeing how tall and slim I was compared to his short, stocky stature. I just wanted to crawl under a rock. This is not how things happened in my Danielle Steele novels.

Finally it was over. We got into a waiting car and departed right away. Devin didn't want to greet anyone. He just wanted to go to the reception at the church hall and get a beer. It was budget catering, with bologna and cheese sandwiches on paper plates and piles of potato chips covered with Saran wrap. I could see people complaining and saying, "What the hell is this?" Music was blasting from Devin's huge stereo. I told him I couldn't dance because of my neck. He said that was fine and took off with his buddies.

Most of the guests left early to go to a restaurant because they were hungry. Devin and his friends stayed and kept knocking back the beers. By the end of the evening he was too drunk to walk and sat motionless in a chair until his friends helped to put him in the passenger seat of my car.

We were booked into the Poconos Cove Resort in the heart of the Poconos New Hampshire Mountains for three nights. I had to drive there in the dark using a map with Devin passed out in the passenger seat. It was pouring with rain and I was driving around the mountains in the middle of nowhere, completely lost. It took me four hours to find the hotel, after stopping many times to read the map using the interior car light.

I nudged Devin's arm when we finally reached our destination. He woke up and dragged his twelve-pack of beer off the backseat while I checked us in. The supervisor at the front desk gave me a funny look because the groom was supposed to take care of that. Our room had a huge heart-shaped tub in the middle of the floor. Romance was the last thing on Devin's mind. He got into the bed with his beer and started watching TV. He asked me to join him but I didn't want to. The smell of booze was making me nauseous.

As I wouldn't cooperate he pulled out his gun, grabbed my hair and made me give him a blowjob, with his finger on the trigger the whole time. He was so angry and slapped me across the face because I kept vomiting over him. When it was over I went to cry in a chair and prayed he'd fall asleep soon.

He finally fell unconscious watching TV. I didn't want to sleep with him so I lay on the hard, ceramic bathroom floor covered in towels to keep me warm, looking up at the ceiling, with tears dripping down the side of my face. In the early hours I went to join him so he would wake up thinking I'd been there the whole night.

I was holed up in that room while he drank beer morning, noon and night for three days. We didn't hike in the mountains like other couples. He watched TV the whole time. I had to get food from the machine in the hallway to survive. Then I'd go back to the room and watch him empty one beer after another. I wanted to go home. Then it hit me. Home was now the basement apartment in Mary's ranch house.

Our married life started out with Devin working for his landlord, doing yard and construction work. Then he heard rumors that two or three men in suits carrying guns were asking where he was. He looked at me across the kitchen table and said,

"I don't know what to do and how we're going to hide. I'm tired of moving around. They're a very dangerous mafia group and will cut our legs off and get away with it for sure."

"What about me going to college out of state? Vocational rehab will pay for everything and the drug dealer will never find us if I go to Gallaudet University. What do you think?"

"That's a great idea. Let's do it."

Chapter 46

The following month we traveled to Washington D.C. with his foster parents to look at apartments and to get me registered at Gallaudet University. We looked at an apartment in a mainly black neighborhood. It was very clean and not too bad. As we were leaving, two black kids started calling Devin names. He got irate and started throwing rocks at them. His foster father Jim took him by the neck and put him in the car, telling him he would get reported for assaulting a minor. Devin yelled out of the window, calling the kids niggers and monkeys. I was mortified and slid down into my seat so no one could see me.

Jim told the realtor to find an apartment in a white neighborhood. We followed him to a town further out from Gallaudet University and to a great apartment on the third floor of a tall red brick building. It had huge windows and dark antique wood everywhere. I loved it. We put down a deposit and were set to move into it in two weeks.

Devin got a full-time job with an alarm company through a friend, checking people's houses when their alarms went off. I was shocked because he had a long criminal record so they must have hired him without doing a background check. He was even cockier now because he got to wear a uniform and looked like a policeman. I was happy he was working nights because it meant I didn't have to sleep with him.

My parents gave us some hand-me-down furniture and we settled into our new apartment with my dog Coco. This time Devin put three padlocks on the inside of the door. I asked him why he was doing that. He looked at me and said, "I don't trust you. I'm going to lock you up when I go to work at night."

Devin looked at my classes schedule and worked out how long it would take me to get back and told me I had to wear a watch at all times. If I was more than five minutes late he said he'd shoot the dog. I said, "What about rush hour traffic or roadworks or accidents?"

He screamed, "I don't care! That's your problem. The dog is getting killed no matter what." He told me he'd be watching me to see if I was talking to other guys. I was so anxious and always checking outside to make sure he wasn't spying on me. He had made friends at work who would give him rides whenever he wanted and it was such a vast campus he could easily blend in unnoticed.

I took care of Coco like a baby and trained her to go potty on newspaper on the bathroom floor when Devin locked us up. I became so attached to that dog. She was beautiful, with thick black hair like a lion's mane and dark-blue eyes. I treated her like a human being because I had no one to talk to. I realized years later that Devin was very clever by getting me that puppy. It was another way of controlling me by threatening to kill her if I didn't come back within fifteen minutes whenever he sent me to get his cigarettes. I had to run all the way there and back.

The two Asian men who owned the convenience store two blocks away could see the panic in my eyes when I rushed in and often asked me if I wanted them to call 911. Sometimes I had to cut in the line and say it was an emergency, checking my watch all the time and worrying that he'd kill Coco like he had killed Carrots. My hands would always be shaking by the time I got back. I'd open the door to the apartment and see Devin sitting on the couch holding my whimpering dog. I'd grab her, give him his cigarettes and escape to the bedroom. This routine happened every night.

I got a full-time job working at McDonalds up the street from our apartment. I did the opening shift at 4am until 1pm. Then I went to school late in the afternoon, depending on my schedule. I also worked early mornings at the weekends so I could have three days off during the week.

My parents wanted me to come home for Thanksgiving and told me they would pay for my plane ticket but not Devin's. To my surprise he was happy to let me go. For a few weeks now he'd been working consecutive nights. I suspected he was seeing someone and I didn't care. Hopefully he'd leave me for good.

My neighbor, Molly, said she would look after Coco, and Devin said, "Thank god, because I have no patience with that dog. I'm glad she'll be out of my sight."

He drove me to the airport early in the morning. Just as I was getting out of the car he said "Jennifer" three times. Then he warned, "You'd better not be with any guys behind my back or you know what I'll do."

I grabbed my suitcase and hurried into the airport, glancing back to make sure he was really gone. I felt so free! My parents picked me up at Boston Logan International Airport in the baggage claim area because it was so cold outside. My mother was not happy to see me wearing worn-out clothes and no boots.

On Thanksgiving Day I saw my cousins Kristen and Jamie. They were happy to see me but horrified at how skinny I was. They asked if I was eating okay. In fact, there were many times when there was no food in the apartment and I'd survive on yellow tomatoes from Oscar, the old man who lived in the apartment under ours. I'd open the window and yell down to him, telling him I couldn't come down because I was locked up inside. Oscar had a genius idea. He'd put the tomatoes in a basket, tie a rope to it and throw it up. I'd catch the rope and reel the basket up to my window. Then I'd drop the basket back down and shout, "Thank you so much!"

I didn't want my Thanksgiving weekend to end and I cried in my childhood bed the night before I had to leave. My parents dropped me off at the airport. It was an emotional goodbye. My dad said he was so proud of me going back to college and trying to make something of my life.

I was supposed to arrive at Maryland airport at 7:20pm. I was expecting Devin to pick me up at 7:30pm. I waited at the curb. It was 8pm and he still wasn't there. Dad had given me fifty dollars so at least I had money for food. At 9pm I asked someone to call Devin for me because I couldn't hear the payphone. The stranger told me his phone kept ringing and there was no answer. So I went back to the airport to get something to eat at McDonalds.

It was after 11pm when I went back outside to wait for him. I just knew he would be driving drunk and I didn't want to go in his car. Finally he showed up, driving very fast and almost hitting the edge of the sidewalk next to me. My hands started to shake. I opened the door and the stench of alcohol hit me. He yelled at me to get in the car. He was sitting half bent over the wheel with his eyes almost shut. I told him I would drive home. He whipped out his pistol and shouted, "Get in or I'll shoot you!"

He drove at more than 100mph on the highway and wove in and out of the lanes. My heart was pumping so hard. I screeched, "Watch out!" multiple times. I even grabbed the steering wheel when he was about to hit someone. He slapped me hard on my hand and laughed. Once we arrived, he fell forward over the steering wheel. I hauled my suitcase off the backseat, took the car keys from the ignition and left him comatose on the front seat.

Molly had dropped Coco back to Devin earlier because she knew I was going to be home soon. I panicked because she didn't come to me when I called her name. I found her in the bathroom cowering under the sink. There were feces on the newspapers, no food and the water bowl was empty. I knew something had happened to her while I was gone. I looked in the kitchen and was shocked to see hundreds of empty red-and-white Budweiser beer cans on the floor and in the sink. Then I saw pink lipstick marks on the dining room wall. I never wear pink lipstick. I ran into the bedroom to see if my things were still there. My bedside drawer was half open and some underwear and bras had been thrown in that weren't mine, and a perfume bottle I'd never seen before was on the dresser. Someone had been here the whole weekend!

I got up early and looked out of the window to see my white car was still parked outside. He must still be passed out in there. I cleaned up the bathroom with disinfectant and threw the empty beer cans out. Then I heard someone bashing on the door. It was Devin. He was enraged that I'd left him in the car. I told him I couldn't carry him up three floors and said that I knew that he was cheating on me.

"You were with another girl!" I shouted. "Why are you keeping me here? Go be with her and get rid of me. I want a divorce!"

He screamed at me to shut up. Then he said my name three times. "I'm not going anywhere. I'm staying with you."

Chapter 47

I would never know when Devin would be back. Sometimes he'd leave me locked inside the apartment for days. He'd broken my TTY telecommunication machine so I couldn't contact anyone. I had to lay newspapers in the hallway for Coco because I couldn't take her outside to go to the bathroom. The apartment smelled so bad. I'd kill time by doing my homework or playing Nintendo. But mainly I'd lie on the floor next to my dog. She tilted her head like she could understand and followed me around the apartment. She even got on the couch next to me, put her paws on the back of the couch and looked out of the window with me.

I noticed that Devin would put even more spray deodorant on his private parts than usual before leaving for work. I realized later that this habit of his was why I kept getting urinary tract infections. It was obvious to me that he was seeing someone at work or after work. I wondered if he was making her ill too.

Every morning he would come home stinking of beer, slump on the couch and say, "Hey, do you want go to bed with me?" I always refused, unless he got his gun out. Then I'd have to give him a blowjob before I went to school. He'd be done in five minutes and I'd run to the bathroom and brush my teeth to get rid of the disgusting taste.

One Friday night I was locked up again, thinking I'd be there for the whole weekend watching TV with Coco. It was around 2am and I was sitting in the brown leather recliner with Coco next to me. I heard a loud knock at the door and looked through the peephole. Devin was standing outside with blood all over him. I started shaking. Maybe he'd got into a fight again or chopped someone's fingers off. He slid the padlock keys under the door and shouted for me to hurry up and let him in.

He stumbled in and I was hit by the strong smell of booze. He immediately went into the bedroom to get his .45 pistol, put his finger on the trigger and pointed it at my head. Coco ran into the bedroom to hide. I tried to calm him down by saying, "Please don't shoot me. What's happened to you?" I knew if I snapped at him he would shoot me in an instant.

"You've got to help me," he said breathlessly. "I killed someone. I ran him over 'cos he tried to take my money without giving me my weed. I dragged his body into the woods. That's why I've got blood all over me. The car's wrecked. It's in the parking lot. You've got to help me move it so I can report it stolen," he garbled.

I thought I was going to have a heart attack. My whole body was quaking with fright. It was pitch black and raining. I said adamantly, "No! I'm not doing it."

"Fine. I'll shoot you and your dog." He gave me the car keys. "There's no one around. We can hide the car and no one will know. I'm not going to jail because of that thieving punk."

We hurtled down the stairs and out into the parking lot. I was shocked to see the front windshield was shattered and there were huge dents on the hood and the front bumper. I got in the driver's seat. He sat beside me with his gun pointed at my head and told me to start the car and drive. But I couldn't see anything in front of me.

He nudged the gun at my shoulder. "Drive!" he screamed, "Or I'll shoot your head off!" Then I noticed what appeared to be hair and skin hanging from the top of the shattered windshield near the rearview mirror. It was a partial human face! I was horrified but I couldn't react because Devin was urging me to move the car. Forced to drive blind, I rolled down the window and peered out to try to see where I was going. I remembered the parking lot and the street layouts because I stared at them all the time with Coco from the apartment window.

I drove up the hill. There were no cars coming, so I turned right, went halfway down the street and pulled over. Then I got out and ran back to the apartment, with him limping behind me. I arrived first and cried on the living room floor, with Coco licking my face. Devin came in later and told me to get up and find some scissors. The dog growled so I yelled at her to go in the bedroom but she wouldn't budge.

"I'm going to kill that dog. She's got a bad attitude," he said, raising his gun to shoot.

I yelled that I'd only help him if he left the dog alone. He backed off so I put Coco in the bedroom and shut the door. Devin took off his sweatshirt and told me to cut it up into pieces and flush them down the toilet while he took a shower.

It took me more than two hours to cut up that material. His hoodie was so thick and the scissors were so blunt they hurt my fingers and gave me blisters. Devin took his bloody jeans off and threw them in the bin. I don't know why he made me cut up his sweatshirt, when he just threw his bloody jeans away. That made no sense. I went into the kitchen and turned the lights on. He immediately told me to turn them off because the police would be looking for him. Then he demanded that I run to the store to get his cigarettes. It was 4am. I had to be back in fifteen minutes. He held Coco by her collar and forced her to sit next to him on the couch.

Running as if my life depended on it, I got to the 24-hour convenience store and asked for Newport menthols. The two Asian men behind the counter asked if I wanted them to call the police. They had seen me run in like this many times before, but never so panic stricken and in tears. I told them no, paid quickly and started running. I had four minutes left. I could barely get up the stairs because I was so out of breath.

Coco was still alive! Devin smiled and said, "Wow! You made it back on time. I guess you'll do anything for this dog. That's good to know." He took the cigarettes and chain smoked until the early hours of the morning.

I felt so bad for the poor guy who was killed. He must have had a family somewhere. All I know is that he was white and had dark brown hair because of what I saw on the windshield. I tried to get Devin to tell me where he put the body but he refused. He must have dumped it in the woods close to the apartment because he wouldn't have been able to drive far.

While Devin was passed out on the couch I snuck out with Coco to see what was going on with the car. Devin had already reported it stolen and I could see police cars and a tow truck nearby. A police officer and another guy were examining the car and staring at the windshield. Surely they would notice the partial face inside the car at the top of the shattered window.

Back at the apartment I watched them tow the car away, with Coco sitting next to me. Devin started to wake up. I told him about the tow truck. He panicked and told me to get away from the window. He was a nervous wreck.

"This is what happens when you drink and drive," I said foolishly. He slapped my face and told me never to say that again.

The insurance company paid for a rental car while mine was being fixed. We went to the impound lot to see how badly it was damaged. Devin got inside and forced me sit inside with him. Oh my god! I could still see skin and hair attached to the roof next to the windshield. I was astounded that nobody had noticed it. Devin quickly wiped it off with a cloth he found on the back seat.

"Nobody's ever going to know I killed that dude now," he smiled. He was ecstatic that the car was going to be fixed and the insurance covered everything. I was incredulous that no one had seen the gory evidence inside. How could they have missed it?

Two weeks went by and nobody came to arrest Devin. I was so disappointed.

Chapter 48

I had convinced Devin to leave the padlocks off the door so I could take the dog out. She was getting big and her lakes of pee and human-sized poops were stinking up the place.

"I'll kill you if you try and leave. And remember, if you report me and I go to jail I'll come out meaner and kill you and your whole loser family," he reminded me as usual.

It felt so good to be independent without Devin around or locks on the door. I took my dog downstairs for a walk twice a day. The lady who lived on the first floor with Oscar, the old man who gave me the yellow tomatoes, gripped my hand as I was about to leave through the front door.

"I need to talk to you girl. I know you're deaf and mute," she said, using old-fashioned language. "Look at me. We can hear your husband screaming at you almost every night. We know he hits you all the time. Oscar told me to stay out of it. Take my advice. Go to the kitchen or the bathroom or even go to bed to avoid him. Promise me you'll do that next time?" Her words echoed in my mind.

One night I was home alone with Coco, playing Nintendo. I was wearing my long white lacy nightgown that my mother had given me for Christmas. I cherished it because it looked so beautiful on me, with my long dark hair. Suddenly I jumped out my skin, startled by the sound of someone bashing at the door. Devin staggered in stinking of booze. I carried on playing Nintendo with shaking hands. I was petrified he'd grab me or hurt my dog. He sat across from me and stared at my face. I didn't want to play anymore. I remembered the old lady's words and went to the kitchen with my dog, saying I needed to fill her water bowl. Then I put on a long black rain coat over my nightgown, grabbed her leash and said, "You need to go to the bathroom little doggie? Okay. Let's go for a walk."

"Hey! Where do you think you are going? You'd better be back in fifteen minutes or you'll pay the price."

I started walking, checking my watch. Before I knew it, over ten minutes had passed. I quickly turned around and started to run back. "Come on Coco we have to hurry back before he hurts us," I panted.

When we got to the apartment Devin was in the dining room with his .45 gun in his hand, on the phone talking to someone. I could barely breathe because my lungs were bursting from running so fast. I made an excuse to go to another room. Coco had her tail tucked behind her rear, sensing danger. I took her into the bathroom and shut the door. I wasn't allowed to lock it or he would go ballistic. Then I sat on the toilet to pee. Suddenly the door sprang open and Devin stormed in with his gun.

"Hey, I need to go to the bathroom. Please can you wait in the living room," I asked as nicely as I could.

"No. I'm going to kill myself right now and you're going to watch." He aimed the gun at his head. I looked at him and said nothing, which made him angry. So he turned the gun around and pointed it at me. Coco barked at him, so he kicked her across the floor. I screamed at him not to hurt my dog and slid her across the floor to the other side of the bathroom. Devin turned the gun around again and pressed it into his forehead.

"Why are you doing this? Why you want to kill yourself?" I asked tearfully.

"I can't be with my girlfriend because of you. She says you need to be out of my life or she won't see me."

"Fine. I'll divorce you right now! You can have her with my blessing. Let me pack right now and leave."

"No! You can't divorce me. You can't go!"

"But I thought you wanted your girlfriend!"

He left the bathroom and went back to the living room. I was a wreck and shaking so hard. This made no sense. I looked in the mirror and prayed, *Please God, don't let him kill me tonight. He can shoot me in the arm or leg. Don't let it hurt too much.* Coco was whimpering because she knew I was in danger. I wanted to smoke a cigarette so badly so I went to the living room. He was sitting on the couch hunched over. I wondered if I should run out with my dog. He stared at me and then he beckoned me to join him. I told him I was going to bed because I was really tired. It was 2:30am.

"Why don't you watch TV with me and relax?" he said. I pretended to get a drink from the kitchen. Coco followed me with her tail tucked behind. I got into bed and positioned myself on the edge of the mattress, feeling like I was about to fall off a cliff. We had a king-sized water bed with drawers underneath. I felt the water move. Devin tapped me on the back and told me to roll over to face him. Then he switched on the lights. He was on the phone to someone. I put my hearing aids back on and read his lips. He was saying, "I'll take care of her. I'll see you soon." I felt this awful pit in my stomach. I was going to die tonight. He lay down on his side and fixed his eyes on me. There was something different about his expression. He was calm and more intense.

"Please. I need to go to sleep. It's late," I said, trying to hide my anguish. He grabbed my right hand and told me to take my wedding ring off. How could I do that without my right? He squeezed my fingers together as if he was trying to break them. I tried to release the ring on my left hand using my thumb and finally managed to push it off. I knew he was going to kill me. All I could do was sign 'I love you.' He smirked and said "Jennifer" three times in his satanic, weird voice.

"You're not happy being married to me. Don't pretend," he said, then put the pillow over my face and held it down. I tried to push him off but it was impossible. The only way to stop this was to pretend I was dead. So I lay there, not moving a muscle. He slowly removed the pillow and realized I was still alive. So he resumed his position of lying on his side staring at me. Then he took the gun from his back pocket and aimed it at my heart with his finger on the trigger. I remember every detail as clearly as a slow-motion movie.

"NO!" I screamed, using my right hand to swipe the gun away. There was a loud bang. I saw smoke coming from the pistol barrel. I stared at it, then looked behind me at the white wall. It was covered with red splatters. I tried to figure out whose blood it was. Then I looked down at my white gown and felt a river of warmth pouring from my shoulder. Thirty seconds later I was hit by the most excruciating pain. It was like a train had run over my arm. I screamed in agony at the top of my lungs.

"Please call 911 so I won't die. Please!"

Devin put the gun back at my head and said, "Sorry. I have to finish you off. You'll tell everyone what I did."

"No! I promise I won't say anything. Then thinking fast, I said, "I'll say you were cleaning your gun and it accidentally went off. Please let me live!" I was crying so hard because I was thinking of my parents and my brother. I wanted to see them again. And I'd never have children if he killed me now.

"Okay. I have to carry you to the living room and put you on the couch. Nobody cleans their gun in the bedroom." He lifted me up out of bed with my right arm hanging down. I couldn't feel any nerves or muscles. I asked him to put my arm on my stomach because I was too scared to touch it. Then he dumped me on the couch. I screamed in pain and watched as he ran to the bedroom door to get the phone. Blood was gushing out everywhere on the floor, on me and on the couch. I kept losing consciousness but I forced myself not to black out because I didn't trust him.

I kept thinking of all the good times I had had with my family: camping, canoeing with my dad on the lake, the sailboat, walks on the beach, playing in my grandparents' basement with my brother Antonio, fishing with my dad off Duxbury bridge ... all these good memories kept me alive. Coco had run out of the bedroom when the gun was fired and was hiding in the kitchen. Once Devin was gone she came over to me, whimpering when she saw me hurt with blood everywhere.

The gunshot was so loud I thought one of the neighbors must have called the police by now. I could hear Devin telling the operator his wife had been shot by accident. My white gown was soaked and blood was still gushing out. It was so painful and my right arm was paralyzed. I was terrified at the thought of losing my arm and being unable to sign. I tried so hard not to fade away but when I opened my eyes I saw darkness closing in.

Devin ran out and greeted the policemen, pretending to be distraught. I saw two of them holding their guns in the air, checking all the rooms. One of them looked at me and his face turned white when he saw me on the couch, with blood spreading out all over my white pajamas. I suddenly felt the fear leave my body.

"Please help me. Please help me," I asked him tearfully.

He snapped out of his trauma and put his hand on my arm and said, "Everything will be alright. People are coming to help you." He looked at Devin and ordered him to go to the end of the hallway. Then he radioed everyone to let them know it was safe to come in. Around a dozen first responders flooded the room and stared at me in shock. I'll never forget one handsome fireman in his yellow pants with suspenders, brown jacket, and boots up to his knees. He had a gentle smile on his face and looked at me in a caring way.

He said, "I'll take care of you, don't worry."

I looked at him and said, "Please don't go. Stay here with me." He held my hand while a medical technician taped gauze over the bullet hole to stop the bleeding. The fireman helped to get me off the couch and onto the stretcher. I cried because it was too painful to move.

He said, "Look me in the eye and hold on to me. I'll stay with you." I gazed into his dark eyes and moved my legs over from the couch to the stretcher. The first responders wrapped bandages around my chest once I was upright. I didn't want to let go of the fireman's hand. He stayed with me the whole time.

Suddenly Devin walked in with two police officers. "I'm so, so sorry," he cried hysterically.

I scowled at him and refused to say anything. A paramedic said, "You should say something to make him feel better. He's really upset."

The handsome fireman sensed it wasn't an accidental shooting and ordered, "Get that guy out of here!"

They had to carry me down three flights of stairs to get me to the ambulance. The fireman gripped my hand while five other firemen carried the stretcher carefully downstairs. Outside in the dark, a crowd of neighbors had gathered to watch me being taken out on a stretcher. They gasped as I went by and waved and blew me kisses. There were police cars and fire trucks everywhere. I looked at the fireman as he got into the ambulance and pleaded with him not to let Devin come with me. I was scared he would kill me outright. He told me not to worry. He was being questioned by the police.

I was rushed to the emergency room at Prince George's Hospital. The fireman had to let go of my hand when the nurses took over. I cried because I was terrified, wondering what was going to happen. There were around seven people working on me under the bright lights. They cut my beautiful white pajamas and underwear off and started jabbing my body with needles. I was hooked up to an IV and a urine tube was put in. Then I was given some shots.

The X-ray machine arrived and the doctor took some images of my right shoulder. He looked at me with concern and said, "Don't worry. I'm going to take care of you."

I felt safe with him and replied, "Can you be my doctor?" His name was Dr. Alzamora. He smiled and said that he could.

I was in so much agony they had to give me more shots as they applied the bandages. Dr. Alzamora called my dad at 3am and told him I'd been shot. My dad instructed him not to give me any blood transfusions because he had seen an episode of *60 Minutes* on TV and was worried I would get AIDS. The doctor told him it would take longer for me to recover without transfusions but my dad said he didn't care, they weren't allowed to do it.

The police called my dad and told him Devin was at the police station. My dad blurted out right away that Devin had tried to kill me and he just knew this was attempted murder. All they had to do was talk to me in the emergency room. A few minutes later a policeman came in with a nurse.

"Did he try to kill you or it was an accident?" he asked bluntly. Everyone stopped working on me, including the doctor and the room fell silent.

"Yes. He tried to murder me." The policeman ran to the phone on the wall to have Devin arrested. Dr. Alzamora looked at me and smiled.

"I'm proud of you for telling the truth. Most women would be too scared to do that. You did the right thing."

I was sure I was free from Devin. Now he'd be jailed for ten years at least.

Out in the hallway two policemen were guarding the door and making sure no unwelcome visitors came into my room. I saw my mother being held up by my dad and a nurse because she was too weak to walk. My dad went pale when he saw me all battered up with bruises, with dried blood in my hair. I cried when I saw how devastated they both looked and said I was sorry to have put them through hell for the past four years.

My dad looked at me said, "I'm proud of you." I didn't understand how he could be proud of me. Look at the mess I'd gotten them in. "I'm proud of you for telling the truth and telling the police he tried to murder you." Blood was coming out of his nose. The nurse told him to sit down so she could take his blood pressure. It was extremely high. My mom was crying and telling him to calm down.

"I'm okay, really," I tried to reassure them. "I'll fight through this and start over."

I suddenly remembered that Coco was all alone in the apartment. What if Devin was let out of the police station and he killed her? My dad said he would go back in the morning, pick up the dog, collect my stuff with a U-Haul and talk to the landlord about changing the locks. After a couple of hours they left and checked into a nearby hotel. It had been their Northeastern University football team reunion party that night. Mom had prepared casseroles and appetizers the night before. I felt so bad that I had ruined their evening.

I had to be transferred to another room. It was agonizing every time I was moved. Every little bump made me yell out in pain. A tall, good looking nurse called Brian told me I was going to be okay. Every time the trolley hit a bump I cried out in pain. "Please be careful," I said over and over in tears. The worst part was going in the elevator. There was a massive jolt when the wheels hit the sliding door tracks. My arm was killing me. Brian consoled me and patted my hair down.

Finally I arrived in my room. I was laid down flat and couldn't move because of the intense, tortuous pain. It was constant. I felt like I was on fire. I cried out for someone to help me and do something. Brian said he could give me Tylenol and that was all.

"Why aren't I getting pain medication? Tylenol does nothing. Why can't you give me something stronger?" I discovered later that my godfather Tom had told my parents not to allow me to have any narcotics because he'd seen so many people get addicted to them. The instructions were no pain medication, just Tylenol.

I started to hurl things from my hospital table. I threw my blanket off because it hurt so much. A nurse came rushing in and gave me a sleeping pill to calm me down. When I woke up my parents were sitting in my room. All of sudden the pain came back. I couldn't stand it. It was like a thousand knives being twisted in my flesh. I started to cry and scream. My parents were startled and bolted upright in their seats.

"I can't take this! Please kill me now! I can't take this pain!" I yelled so loud that the patients and all their visitors in the curtained-off rooms next to me could hear. A male nurse came running in to try to calm me down. I was kicking and making so much commotion it was obvious I needed something stronger than flu medication.

He looked at my parents and said, "You really can't worry about her being addicted to pain meds. Look at the poor girl. She's in unbearable pain. Please let us give her something stronger so she can be comfortable and heal."

Finally my parents agreed. The nurse immediately called the doctor to get my order in. He came in ten minutes later and said, "I'm going to give you Demerol. It's one of the best pain medications we have." I felt something sharp going into my butt and all my suffering melted away in seconds. Finally I could breathe! A whoosh of ecstasy went through every cell of my body and all my torment disappeared.

My parents looked on in amazement. I thanked the nurse. He smiled and told me I would be getting pain relief every two hours. An hour and forty-five minutes later the sharp pain came back. My mom pressed the buzzer for the nurse and said, "She's suffering again. Please can you give her something." The nurse explained that they had to wait exactly two hours on doctor's orders. I counted the minutes down to the second until two hours had passed. Then the nurse administered another shot. This kept going on all day and all night with me watching the clock until my next dose of pain meds arrived.

The doctor came in and explained my X-ray results. The ball and socket joint in my shoulder and my arm bones had been shattered into hundreds of tiny pieces. The bullet had just missed my heart. One millimeter to the right and I would have died without question. My dad told me he had spoken to the orthopedic surgeon, who wanted to amputate my arm because it was so irretrievably shattered. The other option was to take some bone from my hip and make one arm shorter than the other.

I shrieked, "No! I don't want my arm to be cut off. No!"

My dad said, "Dr. Alzamora told us he can't let you go home because your iron is way below normal and you're in a lot of pain so you can't be moved. Since you didn't get the blood transfusions it's going to take longer to move you. They're going to put more bandages on you until you're transferred. I'm not letting anyone make decisions about your arm until I talk to a doctor at Boston General."

"Okay," I said. "I hope they can save my arm. I don't want another disability."

The following day two detectives came into my room and asked me endless questions. They wanted to know how I got involved with Devin and why I stayed with him. They had read his criminal history and psychiatric reports and found more guns hidden in the attic. They asked me if I was aware of them. They had also found a phone number written on a bit of paper in his pants and called to see who it was. It was his secret girlfriend.

My mom looked at me angrily and asked, "Why the hell did you stay with him?"

I screamed and threw glasses across the room. I was so mad that I didn't get help sooner. I wasn't brave enough to tell anyone what that monster had done to me. I told everyone to get out. Then the nurses came running in to give me a sedative. How clever he was to have kept me as his captive for so many years.

A week went by and my pain medication was stretched to every three hours instead of every two. The phone rang and my mother answered it. Her face turned ashen.

"What's going on? Tell me please." She told me Devin had been released from jail because it was overcrowded. I burst into tears. I couldn't believe it. How could they let him go after what he did to me?

"But he tried to kill me!" I shouted. Now I was paranoid. He could easily get into the hospital during the night and shoot me dead. Mom told me it was the judge's decision to let him out on bail until the court proceedings. There was enough evidence to make sure he went to jail for twenty years or more. She said the police would take my name off the patient list and replace it with something else and a police officer would guard my door at all times. The nurse had to give me another sedative.

My dad and his best friend Tom loaded up a U-Haul with my stuff and my dog Coco. Dad put the bloody couch in the dumpster and cleaned the place up because he wanted the security deposit back. He told me it was a harrowing scene, with blood splattered on the walls and all over the bedroom. It must have been so distressing for him to clean up his daughter's blood.

He also found the Polaroids of me that Devin had taken at the halfway house. I couldn't image his reaction to those and just felt appalled.

Dad drove over to Gallaudet University to let my friends and professors know what had happened. News of my injury spread all over the campus and soon I had visitors and piles of get-well cards. Everyone was dismayed at the sight of my bandaged arm and all the dried blood in my hair. I read their messages and felt comforted that all these people cared about me.

The next day my mom was sitting with me when the phone rang. During the call she rushed to turn on the TV. Devin was standing on the window ledge of a hotel threatening to jump off. There were police everywhere and the street was blocked off, leaving the cars in front of the hotel stranded for hours.

"The police are on the phone," she said. "They're asking if you would talk him out of killing himself. He says he wants to speak to you."

I looked right at her and said, "Tell him to go to hell and die!" He was always threatening to kill himself and was never successful at it. He just wanted attention. Later on the news it was confirmed that after a four-hour stand-off the police had convinced him to step away from the ledge. He was taken to a mental institution for help.

A couple of days later, my mother came into my room with my watch in her hand. She placed it on the hospital tray next to me. I stared at it in horror, picked it up with my left hand and threw it hard against the wall, screaming, "I'm never wearing a watch again!" She dashed out into the hallway and three nurses came running in. One of them gave me a shot in the arm to calm me down.

To this day I haven't worn a watch in over twenty-five years.

Chapter 49

Several weeks had gone by and my pain was getting better, but I still needed pain medication every four hours. Dr. Alzamora came in to speak to me.

"You've got to eat more greens to get your iron levels up so you can go home. You need to walk around too. You haven't been out of bed since you arrived."

I looked at him and said, "I can't get up and walk. It's too painful."

"You can do it, I know you can. You need to walk first before I can get you transferred to Massachusetts General Hospital."

The next morning I asked my favorite nurse Dave to help me. I felt sore all over and weak from not getting up for so long. I swung my legs over to the side of the bed. The bandages were so heavy and it was hard to move. I felt like a giant with a disabled arm.

Dave said, "You can do it. Come on, let's get you standing up." I tried to stand up by holding on to him but it was too painful. I only took a few steps before I had to go back to the bed. I was crying, exhausted and out of breath. I needed a pain shot because I was in such agony.

After a few more long days I realized I needed to get out of there so I could start my new life of freedom. I was looking forward to seeing my old friends and my family, and I missed my dog Coco so badly. I kept looking at her photo. So one night I decided to get out of bed. I made my way to the hallway and kept on walking, with a limp, the weight of the bandage pulling me down. I passed a nurses' station and one of the nightshift nurses ran up to me and said, "I can't believe you're walking this far."

"I'm a fighter. I will not give up. I want to get out of here," I told her. She smiled and said I should turn around and try not to do too much. I walked all the way back to my room, sweating but triumphant.

The next morning Dr. Alzamora came to see me. "Hey, you're looking great," he said. "Now that you're mobile I'm going to discharge you. You can go home on Friday." I hugged him. He smiled and said, "You can make it. Have a good life out there."

My mother immediately called my dad and he started arranging flights. I was going to have to sit on the front row because of the huge bandages wrapped around me and I couldn't be touched because the injury still hurt like hell.

The day I was leaving, the male nurse, Dave, came in and gave me a hug and wished me good luck back home in Boston. Then he gave me some pain pills so I'd be relaxed for the plane ride. I felt so sick in the car on the way to the airport and wanted to throw up. My mom was worried because I looked so pale. She asked a stewardess at the ticket desk if someone could help push my wheelchair and get our cases to the door. Everyone was staring at me because of massive bandages on my arm and shoulder. I felt really bad when I got to my seat. Take-off was the worst part because of all the vibrations, which sent waves of pain through my body.

When we arrived in Boston my dad was waiting for us on the runway with a wheelchair. My parents were worried because I looked so ill. I was too sick to talk during the hour-long journey home. Coco jumped all over my legs when I entered the house. I went into the living room and sat in my favorite orange recliner. I was finally home again. I didn't have to worry about Devin locking me up, forcing me to have sex, timing every move or putting a gun to my head. My dog lay on the floor next to me and wouldn't move.

Packages, cards and flowers started arriving. I even received a box full of homemade chocolate chip cookies from a childhood friend in Connecticut. There were so many get-well wishes I couldn't believe it. Then I saw an envelope with a Maryland return address sticker I didn't recognize. It was a letter from Devin. He wanted me to go back to him and said he was sorry for shooting me.

I screamed, "Mom!" over and over again. She came running in and asked me what was wrong. I told her I had received a letter from Devin and I couldn't read it. I asked her to report him for harassment. Mom called the police because he had violated the no contact restraining order that had been granted by the court in Maryland.

"Tell him to go to hell! I don't want to get anything from him ever again!" I cried. From then on my parents opened all the cards before they gave them to me.

Later that day my grandparents came to see me. I was so nervous because I knew they were both angry about what had happened to me. Grandpa Bruno peeked around the living room door and said, "Oh my god! I am so glad you are okay," and some other stuff in Italian. Then he came over and kissed me on the head.

Grammy Bruno came in crying. "Thank god you're alive and well!" They asked me why I hadn't listened to their warnings. I couldn't explain that I'd deceived them to keep them safe. I let my parents keep them company. With the pain medication every four hours I was always dozing off, so I couldn't talk much anyway.

"Listen to me. You need to find someone better than that crazy guy! I told you he was bad news," Grandpa Bruno said, waving his hands around and shouting to my parents about the shrimp loser who shot me. I couldn't wait for him to stop talking about it. Eventually my Grammy told him to shut up.

I couldn't feed myself very well and had to eat with my left hand, with help from my mother. She had taken time off work to look after me. Her boss was very generous and told her to take all the time off she needed on full pay. She didn't go back to work for three months. I couldn't be left alone because I was terrified that Devin would storm into the house and kill me. He had nothing to lose now. I freaked out when the door was left unlocked and constantly looked through the window from my orange recliner to make sure no one was parked outside the house. Devin had told me so many times that he would kill me if

I told the police about him. I couldn't relax until he went to jail for good.

I hadn't seen my brother Antonio yet because he was at Northeastern University in Boston as a freshman. He was coming home at the weekend to see me for the first time. My mother told me he had wanted to fly down to Maryland to visit me in hospital but she had insisted that he focused on school. When he finally came home I cried.

Antonio leaned over and gave me a hug. "I can't believe what happened to you," he said. "I got the news from mom that you'd been shot. I couldn't concentrate in school after that. I was so bothered by it. I wanted to buy a gun and shoot that asshole but my friends stopped me. I was gutted that my sister nearly got killed. I couldn't get over it."

Mom told me later that she regretted not letting him travel down to see me.

Chapter 50

My parents received a referral recommendation from Dr. Hendren, a family friend who also lived in Duxbury. He was the first surgeon in Boston to separate Siamese twins and wrote a book about it. Dr. Hendren recommended that I met with Dr. Pierce, a shoulder specialist at Massachusetts General Hospital. My arm had still not been repaired because my dad didn't want the surgeons in Maryland to amputate or shorten it. That's why I was in so much pain. My shoulder was full of pieces of broken bone.

Dr. Pierce was friendly and encouraging and said there were other ways to fix my arm. I went downstairs to get an X-ray so he could decide what to do. The technician told me to stand against the wall. I told him I couldn't stand up straight and hold my arm up with my other arm, I was just too weak. I screamed for help. My dad came running in.

"I can't do this. It's too painful," I cried.

My dad said he would hold me up while they took the pictures. The technician told him there would be a radiation risk. He said, "I don't care. Please just take the pictures."

After this we were taken to a side room to wait for the doctor. Forty minutes later he walked in and said, "Let me see where the bullet went through. I need to take off these bandages." I had been too scared to look at my injury while I was in the hospital. I imagined there was a wide hole a foot long going through my body. I asked the doctor to describe it. He said, "Take a look. It's only a tiny hole, the size of a dime."

I finally looked down at my right shoulder. It was exactly as he'd described, with black burn marks around it. He turned on the light box on the wall and clipped an X-ray image onto it. I couldn't believe how badly damaged my arm was. The bones were ripped away from the ball socket joint under my shoulder and there was a six-inch gap above my elbow. In between there were hundreds of bits of bone shards. Now I knew why it hurt so much.

"You need serious surgery on your arm right away. I can do it the day before Thanksgiving."

"Oh man. I'm going to miss my turkey dinner," I replied.

He laughed and said, "The hospital's Thanksgiving dinner is really good too."

The doctor explained that I'd need a blood transfusion because it would be more than seven hours of surgery. My dad rejected the idea again, fearful that I'd contract AIDS, so the doctor suggested that family members could donate their blood. My father agreed to the idea.

Dr. Pierce looked at me and said, "The bad news is that your arm will be slightly shorter than the other one." I started to cry. "We have to take some bone from your hip to replace the bone that's missing. There's too much damage in there. I can't repair it." I was so upset that I was going to have another disability. I went home thinking no one would want to be my friend or love me if I looked ugly as well as being deaf. This was going to make everything twice as bad.

My old priest came to the house to pray over me with two of his friends. They all prayed for a miracle that I wouldn't need the surgery. The day before the operation, members of my family and some close church members donated their blood. I was really nervous because I didn't want a shorter arm.

I was transferred to a stretcher bed and the nurses started to prep for me for surgery. As I couldn't move my arm when I was in the X-ray room, Dr. Pierce planned to take more X-rays while I was being put under. I smiled at my parents and said goodbye, then my relatives prepared themselves for a very long wait.

I woke up with bright lights in my eyes and saw Dr. Pierce smiling at me. He had brought a sign language interpreter with him. I said, "Why are you smiling?" He told me a miracle had occurred. Something had happened to my arm that he couldn't explain. When he had taken more X-rays he was shocked to see that the bones were slowly knitting together and I didn't need the surgery after all. My arm was healing itself.

He said, "I only removed some bullet fragments and cleaned things up." I couldn't believe it. How was this possible? Maybe God did answer my prayers with the priest's help.

"My arm won't be short, right?"

"Your arm will be normal and it won't be shortened," he said, smiling.

I cried tears of happiness. My parents were delighted and everyone kept saying that a miracle just happened to me and it was almost beyond impossible that my arm was healing itself. I was only in there for an hour of surgery and not the eight hours that had been scheduled. An occupational therapist had to make a special cast to support my arm. She took measurements and told me she was going to make a plastic support with a sling for me to rest my arm in. The plastic would go around my hips, and my arm would stick out to the front. It couldn't rest my arm against my stomach because the bones were growing together. I even had to sleep with it on to prevent bones fixing themselves in the wrong direction. It was something that nobody had ever seen before and when I wore it in public everyone turned their heads to stare. I felt like a robot, with my arm out in front of me.

The first night I wore it, I woke up at 2am and saw a gun being held above me. I closed my eyes and pulled the blanket over my head. Devin was going to shoot me again. I couldn't breathe. I couldn't move or utter a word for more than one hour. Then I yelled "Dad!" multiple times. The bedroom lights came on but I refused to open my eyes. My hearing aids were off. I felt someone tapping my shoulder but I still couldn't look.

"Devin is in here and he's pointing a gun at me," I cried. I eventually opened my eyes slowly and realized it was my own hand and arm sticking up in the air. My parents got teary eyed when they saw how frightened I was.

"Don't worry," my dad said. "He's not here. He's locked up in a mental institution waiting for the trial. Then he'll be sent to jail for many years, I'm sure of it."

Chapter 51

I couldn't write with my left hand, so I decided to type a letter with one finger using an old-fashioned typewriter. I sent letters to David and Kathy and hoped they'd come visit me. It was depressing sitting in my orange recliner all day watching TV, so I was excited when my mother told me an old high school friend Kathy was coming over from Rhode Island. I cried when I saw Kathy's face. She also got upset at the sight of the weird sling and felt terrible that I was suffering with so much pain. I briefly told her about Devin and his threats. She said she knew something was wrong because I was always crying in class for no reason and I was always late for school.

Around Christmas, David got my letter when he got home from NTID College in New York. He immediately called my mother on TTY and told her he wanted to see me and would come over that evening. When he arrived I had forgotten how handsome he was and his cologne smelt great. He knelt down next to my recliner and gave me the longest hug and kissed my cheek. I was in tears when I saw him. His eyes were watery but he didn't cry.

"I can't believe you almost got killed! I'm so glad you're alive," he said. Then we talked for hours in the living room with my parents peeking in occasionally to see why we were spending such a long time together. David smiled and said, "Hey I've got to take you out of here. You need to get out of the house and out of that chair!"

"Where are you taking me?"

"I'll take you to my family's Christmas Eve party."

"What about my arm in this huge cast. Everyone will stare because it looks so weird."

"Don't worry about that. Everyone would love you to come over."

Wow! David had actually asked me out after all these years! I put on some nice clothes with my mother's help and did my make-up. My dad was a little upset and was against the idea. He said, "I don't think you should go. It's too soon to go out on a date." I told him I needed to get out of the house and David would be going back to New York and I wouldn't see him until the spring. Eventually he agreed to it.

David arrived to take me to his family's party. He was dressed nicely and I felt myself falling in love with him again. I wasn't sure he felt the same way.

"Please be careful with her," my dad told him. "She's very fragile. Don't let her fall on the ice. If she breaks her arm it might have to be amputated."

"Don't worry. I'll take care of her," David said, smiling.

I couldn't wait. This was the first time I had been out of that miserable orange recliner to do something different. It was so cold outside and there was snow and ice on the ground. Coco came out and watched us, whimpering because she didn't trust anyone with me. My parents kept calling for her to come back inside, but she kept nudging my leg with her head. David opened the passenger door and put my seatbelt on. I had my arm in a blue sling against my stomach and had left the plastic cast at home. My parents stood on the porch steps and watched as we pulled out of the driveway.

"Let's go to the park and talk before we go to my house," David said. He drove to Weymouth and parked near a tree overlooking the pond. There was beautiful snow everywhere. Then he turned to me and said, "I've really missed you since high school. When I heard you got shot I was so worried. I was so glad to get your letter when I came home." He held my left hand and leaned over and kissed me on the lips. I felt chemistry and magic, but I couldn't turn towards him because my stupid sling was in the way. I was so frustrated because I wanted to grab his head and kiss him madly. So he pushed my seat back to leave a gap between us and kissed me passionately for ten minutes.

There were cars lined up outside his house and everyone had already arrived. David's nieces and nephews were all running around and hollering. Some of them stopped in their tracks to stare at me. David told them, "This is Jennifer. She's my date." They giggled and ran away. "Just ignore them," he said.

Then his sisters approached us and said, "Oh my, Jennifer you're here." I didn't like them saying my name because it reminded me of Devin's evil chanting. I wanted a new name. Everyone stared as I walked past in my sling.

His mother came out from the kitchen and said, "Oh here you are darling," and kissed me on the cheek. "I'm so glad you are here. David talks about you all the time." She didn't say a word about my arm. I'm guessing David had already told everyone ahead of time not to say anything about it.

He led me to the mistletoe above the door and said, "You know what this means? Come here." He put his arms around me and kissed me, while his nieces watched us, sniggering. "Merry Christmas," he said, smiling at me. He might possibly be my future husband if we keep dating, I thought.

It was finally time to eat. His mom had made the most delicious spread and laid it on the dining room table for people to serve themselves. I was relieved I didn't drop any food with my left hand. After we had finished eating he said, "I have to talk to you about something important." I asked him what was wrong. He said, "My mother told me that she doesn't want me to date you." I asked him 'Why?' in sign language. He said, "Because you almost got killed and your situation is too dangerous to get involved in, especially as he is not in jail yet. My mom doesn't want me to risk it." I was in tears because I really wanted David so badly but he didn't want me.

"Besides," he continued, "I have to go back to school in New York in two weeks." I couldn't believe what was happening. I was so upset that my dream of him being my possible future husband had just evaporated. "But I do know Bob would be interested in dating you," he said, handing me Bob's TTY phone number. But I didn't want Bob. I wanted David. He hugged me and said, "Please try to understand. We can stay good friends. Like brother and sister."

I asked, "So why did you kiss me in the car?" He told me his mother had pulled him into another room while I was in the bathroom and warned him off me. "I will never forget you and I promise if I have a son someday, I will name him David because I'll never forget you," I told him sadly.

We spent the rest of the night watching TV and chatting until he drove me home. My dad came out to the car to help me back into the house. Then he shook David's hand and said, "Thank you for bringing her home safely." I didn't see David for a very long time.

Chapter 52

In February my parents took me to see Dr. Pierce at Boston General Hospital to see if I was ready to wear a regular sling and not the weird contraption they had made for me. He ordered some more X-rays and came back with a big grin on his face.

"Good news! Your bone has grown back together and fused into one. We can take you out of that sling and you can start physical therapy three times a week for two months. But be warned, you can never do any kind of strenuous sport like water skiing or tennis. If your arm breaks, you're in trouble. There's a risk of amputation or serious surgery to try to fix it."

He carefully lifted my arm out of its plastic support and unfastened the hip cast. My arm felt sore and achy because it had been in there for so long. I couldn't lift it or feel anything. I could move my fingers but I couldn't move my arm like I thought I would be able to do. I was in tears and said, "How come my arm is not moving? It's feels like a dead arm to me."

Dr. Pierce smiled. "You have to be patient. With lots of physical therapy you'll regain the use of your arm very soon, I promise you."

I started physical therapy a few days later and learned how to drive with one hand so my mother could go back to work. I dropped her off and picked her up on therapy days. At last, people didn't stare at me every time I went out.

One day a wedding invitation arrived. It was from Scott, an old friend who used to hang out with Devin. Scott was a good kid and had found a wonderful girl to marry. I made the decision to go to his wedding on my own. I sat in the fifth row from the front and was watching the ceremony when suddenly I heard gunfire. I was having a flashback of the time I was forced to marry Devin and how he held a gun to me during the honeymoon. I felt the shock of the loud bang and the bullet going through my shoulder.

Scott was at the altar with his soon-to-be wife and all their beautiful bridesmaids and groomsmen. I looked at them and thought how lucky they were to have a normal relationship while I had spent years being held against my will. Then I started to cry uncontrollably. People turned to look at me as the tears streamed down like a waterfall. I was wailing as if someone had died, and I was interrupting the wedding. "Oh shit," I said to myself and bit down hard on my tongue.

Scott's mother Elaine came and sat down next to me. She put her hand on my leg and didn't say a word. I knew I had to leave because I was disrupting the ceremony and everyone's attention was on me. I used my left hand to say goodbye because I was shaking so badly I couldn't speak. Covering my face I quickly walked out, with all eyes on me. I made it to my car out of breath and in a panic and started howling once more. These people were a painful reminder of my past. I needed to make a new future for myself. I parked my car at a lake and prayed that I would get married to a kind, caring man one day and have many children.

I had spent some time trying to find out where Matt had gone so I could call him on TTY. He was not at Gallaudet when I was there. After several days spent asking if anyone knew his number I realized I had lost him. I had lost my first love forever. So I decided to call Bob. The last time I had seen him was at that party at the motel a few years ago when his girlfriend Lorie clawed his arm because she was furious he was with me. Bob answered right away.

My father threw a fit when I told him I was going out with Bob that night to Uno's Italian restaurant. He yelled that it was too soon and I was still going to physical therapy. I told him I was going crazy sitting in the house all day with just my dog for company and I got ready to go out. My parents were paranoid every time I left the house. Even Coco cried and would lie on the front lawn under the crab apple tree waiting for me to return. She was suffering from post-traumatic stress like me. When anyone tried to approach her she'd run away and hide with her tail between her legs. Everyone thought she was a weird dog. I knew in my heart she'd been beaten by Devin.

Bob looked really happy to see me and felt bad that my right arm was dangling down limply at my side. He was still the tall, handsome guy that I remembered, with thick black hair. I was attracted to him just like I was at high school. He was the dream guy of my romance novels. But I didn't know anything about him now, so it would be interesting to find out what he was really like.

He had arrived in his ugly old pale-yellow Toyota pick-up truck. I didn't like it because he had to use his right hand to operate the shift. It was annoying to feel the grinding metal every time he changed gear and he couldn't hold my hand while he was driving. He took me to Uno's three towns away. We must have stayed there for five hours, talking at the table. Then we went to the bar and shared stories about our families and I explained a little of what had happened to me over the last four years. Bob looked at me and said, "Your smoking is a big turn-off for me. I don't want to date you if you smoke, sorry."

"I'll quit right now," I told him. I've never touched cigarettes from that day on.

I told Bob I despised my name because Devin had always repeated it over to me in a hateful way. Every time anyone called me Jennifer I got chills. Bob asked me what my middle name was. I told him it was Lee. He thought for a moment and said, "Why not call yourself Jennylee?" I immediately fell in love with the name and told my parents and my brother to call me Jennylee from now on. To this day they still insist on calling me Jennifer, even though I went to the courthouse and had it legally changed.

We left the restaurant and went back to Bob's truck in the parking lot. It was January and it was still snowing a little. We kissed and chatted some more before he dropped me back at my house at around 1am. I could hear Coco barking from inside the porch and went in quickly, hoping I wouldn't wake anyone up.

"Why were you out so late? What took so long?" my dad yelled. I told him that this is what deaf people did. They lost track of time and talked for hours. Then I told him Bob was taking me to physical therapy the next day. My parents were annoyed about that too.

Bob arrived on time as promised to take me to Plymouth Rehab and faithfully took me to my physical therapy sessions twice a week. He watched my therapist work on my arm on the floor. I did my best to get through pain by taking narcotics every day.

One day I was lying down with my therapist Julie. She said, "Stretch your hand up into the air." I told her I couldn't do it. Suddenly she screeched, "Look at what you're doing!" I looked up and my right arm was in the air! Bob was clapping. I burst into tears. My therapist shouted, "Victory!" and everyone in the room started to applaud.

Chapter 53

I was feeling very anxious because I had to go to the courthouse to face Devin in a few weeks. I asked a couple of friends from Gallaudet University to support me, and my godfather Tom said he would be there too. My mother took me to the mall to find something appropriate to wear in court. I found a navy-blue dress with gold buttons.

The day of my court appearance arrived. I was dreading it so much I hadn't been able to eat or sleep for days. I had terrible anxiety on the plane to Maryland and awful visions of Devin pulling out his gun in court and shooting everyone. We met with the state attorney on the third floor of the courthouse. She told me I didn't have to testify in court and there would be no jury. My parents were astounded. The attorney explained that Devin's lawyer had agreed to a plea offer from the district attorney to accept five years in jail and twelve years of probation in return for pleading guilty.

"What? That's ridiculous! That's crazy!" I shrieked, crying in disbelief. "He should get more than thirty years in jail for what he did to me. Why do other men get twenty years for selling weed and he's jailed for just five years for almost murdering me?"

I couldn't go down to court because I couldn't stop sobbing. My lawyer told me to stay in her office until they got back. I was so angry that he had gotten away with it. About two hours later, one of my friends returned and said my dad's nose had started bleeding because his blood pressure was so high. They had to sit him at the back of the courtroom in case he had to be rushed to hospital. Then she told me that Devin was with a girl and they were both crying. As he was being led away in handcuffs they both mouthed, 'I love you' to each other, then Devin asked the judge if he could hug his girlfriend. His request was denied and he was taken to jail.

A little later on my parents and my godfather returned. My dad didn't look too good. He told me, "I wanted to go over and strangle that little devil, but Tom said, 'Don't you dare go over there.' I wanted to kill that little punk for what he's done to my family."

For some bizarre reason Tom wanted to take us on a tour of his Secret Service headquarters in Washington D.C. We followed him in our rental car to a ten-story brick building on a busy main road in the city. Once inside we went through a security check and he took us to a secure room where they practiced shooting. I freaked out when I saw the racks of guns and had to get out of there, but my friends wanted to try to hit the targets, with headphones on. I sat in the waiting room, upset that they didn't consider how this would affect me. I couldn't believe it when they started taking pictures of themselves holding a machine gun. It was almost exactly the same weapon Devin had used when I tried to break up with him at his foster parents' house. I felt sick to my stomach.

My mother realized it wasn't appropriate for me to be exposed to all these weapons so we quickly said our goodbyes. I just wanted to go home and get out of Maryland and all its familiar places and distressing memories. We left the following morning.

Chapter 54

My parents had planned a trip to Florida during spring break. Bob wasn't invited and I was pretty upset about that, but I took my TTY with me so I could call him. When we arrived at the timeshare condo I discovered the phone was not compatible with my machine so I couldn't communicate with him for a week, which made me feel miserable.

I decided to sunbathe by the swimming pool. It was a perfect day and not hot at all, so I didn't bother with any lotion. At Sea World the next day my face was swollen up and my nose was so blistered I had to slather it with white cream. The following day I stayed inside the condo recovering from sunburn while my family went to Universal. I couldn't wait to get home to see Bob. I missed him so much.

Shortly after returning to Duxbury, Bob and I were invited to a cookout party at a friend's house. More than thirty people were there hanging out, drinking beers. I panicked and worried that Bob might chat to another girl the way he had done when he was with Lorie, so I held on to his hand tightly everywhere he went.

"Come on. You need to let go of me! I need talk to my friends in sign language," he complained. I got a little mad at him because he didn't understand how much I hated him drinking. I was checking to make sure he didn't get drunk or talk to any girls while I wasn't looking.

A couple of hours later I went inside to use the bathroom. I came out to see him deep in conversation with a beautiful girl. I rushed up to him, grasped his hand and asked, "What the hell are you doing with her?" The girl was shocked that I was so angry and Bob was embarrassed that I was behaving so irrationally. "I can't trust you! You're going to cheat on me! And stop drinking that damned beer!" I yelled.

Bob glared at me furiously. Then he picked up the metal beer keg and threw it at the basement cellar doors nearby to frighten me. Two of his friends grabbed him and led him inside the house. As he was being pulled away, he shouted, "You're a total jerk treating me this way!" I screamed, telling him he could have broken my shoulder. He could have hit me by accident. My fragile shoulder couldn't be touched. One stupid mistake and my arm could have ended up being amputated! I told him I wanted to go home. Bob calmed down, got in the car and apologized for throwing the keg. He was scared to death I'd tell my dad.

I applied for a position at Cardinal Cushing School to work with mentally challenged teenagers as a teacher's assistant. I loved my job. I never told anyone what happened to me and no one noticed my disabled right arm. I kept on taking my pain medication and managed to get through the day. It numbed the agony from my damaged nerves and also helped to dull the memories and flashbacks of my four years of hell.

Most weekends Bob and I would go to parties together. We were invited to a gathering at his friend's house in Scituate on the coast. I was so stressed watching Bob drink. Just like Devin, alcohol made him mean. Out of the blue he started drunkenly swearing at me. That was it. I was done with him. I drove him home, dumped his duffle bag on the lawn outside his house and watched as he staggered off inside. I didn't answer his calls on Sunday. I'm pretty sure he got the message that we were over.

After work I went to the staff parking lot with one of my colleagues. There were red rose petals scattered all over the hood of my car and a note tucked under the windshield. 'Please come back to me. I love you and promise I'll quit drinking. Let me show you how precious you are to me.'

I decided to give him a second chance.

That was a mistake.

*I would like to express special thanks to
Brett Schulman, Scott Porta, Julia Kantecki
and Jackie and David Siegel
for their literary advice and personal support.
Their encouragement finally gave me the strength and
confidence to put my experiences into writing.
I would also like to say a special thank you to my children
who have and always will be my reason for living.
I love you all very much.*

Jennylee Rose Bruno